Political Theory as
Public Confession

Political Theory as Public Confession

The Social and Political Thought of St. Augustine of Hippo

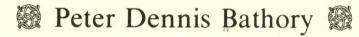 Peter Dennis Bathory

Transaction Books
New Brunswick (U.S.A.) and London (U.K.)

Copyright © 1981 by Transaction, Inc.
New Brunswick, New Jersey 08903

Library of Congress Catalog Number: 80-15667
ISBN: 0-87855-405-X
Printed in the United States of America

Library of Congress Cataloging in Publication Data

Bathory, Peter Dennis.
    Political theory as public confession.

    Includes index.
    1. Augustinus, Aurelius, Saint, Bp. of Hippo—
Political science.   I.   Title.
JA82.B37   320.5'5'0924   80-15667
ISBN 0-87855-405-X

302238

*For Barbara, Eleanor,
and Cecilia*

Table of Contents

Preface

The student of St. Augustine's political thought must be mindful of a number of special problems. Augustine was a pastor preaching regular sermons to his congregation; he was a de facto public administrator in Hippo; and of course, he was a theologian, philosopher, and political thinker. The difficulty for the student of his political thought is that he must be aware that these roles interact in complicated and sometimes confusing ways. This book addresses these issues—focusing on three problems in particular. First, it strives to place Augustine within the proper context of church history, remembering that the church was highly decentralized and lacked the administrative structure of the later Middle Ages. His was not the church of Gregory the Great, let alone that about which St. Thomas wrote. Though Augustine thought and wrote about a universal church, his primary concern was for Roman North Africa in general and Hippo in particular. His devotion to his congregation was integral to all of his thought, from sermons to the most elaborate scriptural exegesis. It was a devotion, moreover, that shaped many of his attitudes toward the politics of the day as well. Thus in reading Augustine, one must take special care to place him in the appropriate historical and geographical perspective.

Second, in trying to uncover his political teaching, this argument stresses the Roman public world that he confronted and in which he participated as a young man. From Augustine's perspective, there were no clear examples of political virtue to be found in that world. The relative virtue and good fortune of Republican Rome had long since sunk under the weight of an elaborate military and bureaucratic apparatus and the superficiality and cultural sterility that accompanied imperial expansion. This presented Augustine with a dual problem. Not only was there a dearth of positive examples to offer to his audience, but that audience, in Augustine's eyes, might as well fall victim to the decadent social and political institutions that governed Rome and Roman culture. Too dependent upon Roman political institutions and language, many North Africans like Augustine and his young friends lacked the ability to discriminate between public good and private interest. In such circumstances, one could scarcely hope to alter the insidious impact of Roman politics and society upon the life of North Africa, no matter how relatively prosperous that world may have been.

Third, this argument recognizes that Augustine's Christian concern for salvation and life in the next world presents difficulties for the student of political thought, for they led him to be suspicious of any earthly regime. His discussion of politics was often cast in critical terms. That positive political thought that one finds in his writing is generally speculative and tentative. If, then, there is an explicit and positive political teaching in Augustine, one must look for it with great care. One should not expect to find such teaching couched in the institutional terms of later medieval discussions of church and state nor in the architectonic terms of the Greeks and Romans.

It is not simply, therefore, a matter of where in his writings one looks for political teaching, but how one looks. Expectations must be shaped with a clear understanding that Christian political thought often stresses the limitations of human action in the *saeculum* and the overriding importance of salvation. They must be further shaped by the specter of a North African bishop confronting the decay of the mighty Roman empire. One must endeavor to understand Augustine's special circumstance to learn from him what is required to reestablish public discourse in a world that has lost touch with anything even approaching agreement about the common good. The Augustine one encounters is, not surprisingly, a thinker who does not reason in the fashion of a St. Thomas or a Cicero. His language is necessarily less explicitly political than either of these thinkers. It is more the language of a sophisticated psychologist—a participant-observer in Roman North Africa and a moral educator. From Augustine's point of view, there was much analysis and education of individuals and communities that would have to take place before anything like a discussion of the public good could commence. Much like Socrates in the *Gorgias,* Augustine felt that the public's business could be properly discussed only by those who had been trained to recognize and overcome the seductive appeals of sophistry. It is, however, more difficult to approach Augustine's discussion of these matters because his argument is not as directly political. The traditional tools of political theory must, therefore, be adapted to account for Augustine's unique perspective as a Christian theologian and a public man.

It is the central contention of my argument that there is a latent political teaching in Augustine. Moreover, his thought and his action constitute an attempt to build the individual and collective foundations necessary to the reestablishment of a more public order. There is no prediction in Augustine, indeed no hint of dramatic or revolutionary change nor of anything approaching a truly just society. There is, however, a constant concern for creating a more just world through the development of a Christian *paideia* or *therapeia*. It is Augustine's effort to this end that will be examined in this book.

To assert that Augustine's is a "political theory as public confession" is to suggest that his is a personal and sometimes obscure political thought. Augustine's intention is never more public than when he speaks of himself. Frequently, when he speaks about public issues, he does so to elucidate questions dealing with the soul. Like Plato, Augustine sought to emphasize the close links between the health and happiness of individuals and the societies of which they are members. Plato responded to questions about the "just soul" with a discussion of the "just state." Augustine, on the other hand, spoke of the pathos of the soul in order to introduce the roots of larger social and political disorders. In confessing his own hope and despair and joy and sorrow, Augustine attempted to awaken in his audience a sense of their limitations as well as their potential as Christians following the dictates of *caritas*. In so doing, he approached the political order hesitantly with a care bred of his own disillusionment with existing political institutions and language.

Ultimately, Augustine attempted to engage his audience in what had been his own search for an individual and collective identity apart from the disastrously incomplete teachings of Rome. In so doing, he introduces what we might call a prepolitical teaching that challenges the foundations of personal and political life.

He sought constantly to educate Roman North Africans so they would be better able to confront the temptations and injustices of Roman politics and society than he and his friends had been in their youth and young adulthood. His own conversion had left him less dependent upon the whim of fickle Roman opinion—more able to judge the rectitude of competing moral claims and in the end freer to act on the basis of that judgment. He hoped that through his teaching, he might offer others a similar freedom.

In order to appreciate Augustine's political thought, one must therefore use his own psychological insight and his own direct comments to his audience as clues to his meaning. Linking the early psychological concerns of his *Confessions* to the political and cultural analysis of the *City of God* thus becomes an integral part of this analysis. This is not a biographical effort like that so brilliantly accomplished by Peter Brown, nor is it an attempt to psychoanalyze Augustine. Rather, it is an attempt to comprehend Augustine—the man and the thinker—through a sensitivity to his personal experience and memories. This background, we must realize, was as critical to his later works, like the *City of God,* as it was to his *Confessions.* Approaching the citizens of an overly extended empire, Augustine employed what Machiavelli might have styled the weapons of an "unarmed prophet." He combined theology, psychology, and political thought in a unique fashion in order to challenge those citizens to reorder their lives. Though some aspects of Augustine's efforts to reorder the world in which he lived may be illuminated by more traditional theological and political analyses, much can also be lost. While this book acknowledges the need for traditional analyses, it also asserts that Augustine cannot be fully understood unless particular attention is paid to his unique psychological and philosophical method.

The primary texts adopted in this project are the *Confessions* and the *City of God.* Others are, of course, critical to the argument, but the systematic nature of these major works, the explicitly edifying purpose of each, and the wide range of Augustine's life experience represented in them commend them as excellent points of departure. Each of these works is, of course, complex in itself, and countless volumes have subjected each of them to detailed analysis. My intention here is less to engage in debates centuries old than to explore in these texts the roots of a political thought couched in language that is often not explicitly political. Previous analyses of his more explicitly political language, especially in the *City of God,* are important as well. This is an effort that extends some of these analyses and challenges others that fail to take seriously enough the positive political teaching implicit in seemingly nonpolitical language.

Earlier works by Peter Brown and Robert Markus have helped shape my thinking on these issues. Brown suggests the importance of linking the *Confessions* and the *City of God* via the tenth book of the *Confessions.* Markus has reminded us of Augustine's concern with human achievement within the *saeculum.* My intellectual debts to these men are great. My personal debts to Professors Paul Ramsey, Samuel Beer,

Norman Jacobson, and William Berlin, each of whom has read this manuscript in one form or another, are even greater. My thanks go to Wilson Carey McWilliams, whose eighteen years as a teacher, colleague, and friend have made all of this possible. And finally, to Anita Neugeboren for her endless patience as a typist and editor.

INTRODUCTION

The Christian Bishop in an Age of Crisis

The true education of the human race, at least as far as God's people were concerned was like that of an individual. It advanced by steps in time, as the individual's does when a new stage of life is reached. Thus it mounted from the level of temporal things to a level where it could grasp the eternal, and from visible things to a grasp of invisibles.

The City of God, X, 14

The world of the Christian bishop had by the time of Augustine become closely aligned with that of the Roman bureaucrat. From the time of Constantius II (337 to 361 A.D.), bishops had joined "the bureaucrats as members of the new governing class." [1] Even more important, they had also become local administrators. Though Augustine's public position was less exalted than the powerful positions of his medieval successors, his place in the ebb and flow of local political issues was unchallenged.[2] With little notice, he became city judge, and his decisions—now bound by the civil law—carried far more authority than those of his predecessors who had relied on church law and apostolic tradition.[3]

With the strength of this official position, Augustine's real force in his North African world could be exerted more easily. Christian bishops like Augustine had learned to be conductors of Roman culture, and Augustine used this skill as well as any.[4] "Christianity," argues Peter Brown, "was able to pass the classical culture of an elite to the

1

average citizen of the Roman world" [5]—to give the average man a sense of participation in his world that the classical rhetor could not. Augustine, however, sought to use his access to this audience in order to educate it to the possibilities of a new moral order. Through conversion, the average man achieved a moral excellence heretofore available only to classical Greek and Roman gentlemen.[6] Augustine saw it as his duty to shape and direct this new found sense of "moral excellence."

The First Principles of Christian Education

The problems Augustine faced, though perhaps made easier by his office and the general appeal of Christianity to the common man, were by no means uncomplicated. He sought, in fact, to redefine the basis of moral excellence. Augustine's plea for moral excellence was a plea for true principles that, he thought, had been lost in the Roman world around him. It was a plea as profound as that of the Old Testament prophet and as sophisticated as that of Plato. His mission was prophetic but in a special sense of that word. He valued the insight of the Platonists but adapted it to an audience that was dramatically different.[7] Likewise, he saw in the prophetic insight an instruction in the renewal of God's people that offered Christians both an example and a sense of historical rootedness. The Platonists lent him psychological insight that informed his own search for truth and molded much of his own edifying mission. The prophets taught him of the passionate force required for a process of social renewal. His power as a teacher and philosopher cannot, however, be found in a study of his adaptation to previous thinkers.[8] It is instead uncovered in an examination of his confrontation with his particular world.

That world dominates his work as a bishop, teacher, theologian, and leader of Roman North Africa. Again, he was the beneficiary of the growth of what Peter Brown calls a "professional clergy," whose primary task had become the maintenance "of the morale of their less educated flocks." [9] But the clergy too had to be guided. It was not enough, Augustine urged, simply to adopt a humble style and to buoy the sagging confidence of the masses. Something had to be done with the congregation, once their attention was gained. They had to be made ready to live in this world, and so had to be protected from dangers within their group and from within themselves as well. Augustine's was not a theology of adaptation. He sought to teach men to become active forces in all aspects of their world.

In the end, Augustine felt that society could continue to exist only if it understood itself. Thus he preached the need to examine the past along with every facet of emotional, intellectual, social, and political experience. He sought not to glorify self-pity nor to enshrine the romantic monuments of the past, but to allow men to free themselves from both. Rome and Roman culture had, he argued, locked men in a sterile past dominated by the dogma of a mythical tradition that encouraged self-deception and prevented creative action.

The past, personal and political, was studied to be overcome. Its hold on the unconscious, individual and collective, was too great to be ignored. People would, however, require new modes of analyzing their pasts if they were to learn of its hold on the present and its control of their lives. New rote answers to psychological, social, and political problems of the day were, for Augustine, no answers at all. Merely to provide a new set of rules and regulations and a new set of offices and officers was to beg the more fundamental question of the atrophy of human will in the face of such offices and officers in Rome. In fact, human nature is such, Augustine suggests, that men need to be kept at the very least anxious about the nature of this new life, lest the pursuit of virtue be blocked by the slothful pursuit of mechanical categories. Augustine sought "the energetic pursuit of virtue." Roman culture had to be stood on its head. The more basic categories of personal, social, moral, and political judgment had to be redesigned.

A Grassroots Revolution

Augustine addressed the provincial and parochial inhabitants of Roman North Africa, not with a sense of the loss of a great tradition, but with the possibility of greatness that lay in the common man. He focused, as did others of his time,[10] on the "hometown" not solely because local ties grew in importance in the face of a decaying empire. More significantly, the formative and reformative action that he sought had to begin on the local level. People had to be awakened to a sense of their own isolation—of the inadequacies of their social institutions and their moral categories alike.

Speaking to Everyman, he asked that each do as he had done. Augustine asked that each look into himself as an individual and as a part of a people. The end of *caritas*—the properly ordered love of God—entailed as well a love of one's self and a love of one's neighbor. He argued in *De Doctrina Christiana* that:

> All . . . men are to be loved equally; but since you cannot be of assistance to everyone, those especially are to be cared for who are most closely bound to you by place, time or opportunity. . . ."[11]

Augustine saw the revival of local chauvinism, in this context, as a challenge to local action and self-definition rather than as a retreat into provincialism.

His task as a teacher was, ultimately, to shift the relevant sphere of action—individual and collective—from the imperial to the local through offering ordinary citizens an alternative explanation of their place—individual, social, and political—within the world of man, the *saeculum*. Augustine thought it necessary to begin with the familiar, and to demonstrate inadequacies even among the most easily accepted assumptions about Roman life held by ordinary people. He hoped thereby to create first the need for a new general explanation, that is, for new formulations of basic but now recognized, shared dilemmas. Then, through a new sort of public discourse, he hoped a new kind of public action would follow.

The church, that is, individual churches and their congregations were to be the vehicles for and provide an arena for such change.[12] Though the proper end of all discourse and action in this life was the next life, Augustine nonetheless sought to influence conduct in this life as well. Earthly peace was needed to encourage social intercourse and to help define the quality of common life within a shared culture.[13] For all of his understanding of the limitations of human institutions, Augustine insisted that they must not be "shunned by the Christian" when they are found to be "helpful to the necessary conduct of this life." [14] Insofar as the temporal peace fosters "a certain coherence of men's wills," [15] it had value. The church's role in this life and for this life, as well as for the next, was to promote peace and the virtues through which peace is to be brought about and sustained.

Augustine recognized, as de Tocqueville would later, that in a period of change when "public morality is destroyed, religious belief shaken and the spell of tradition broken," [16] it was of little use to appeal solely to broad abstractions. In this situation, says de Tocqueville, the problem is that "the country . . . assumes a dim and dubious shape in the eyes of the citizens." It is incumbent upon leaders and citizens alike to recognize that a new order must be founded, based on the "union of private and public interests." [17] Augustine, like de Tocqueville, thought that the potential for such a union—and action based upon it—could be found only in a local arena.

De Tocqueville worried that there could be a drift away from such common action. Augustine described and spoke to a world in which such drift had already occurred. Each man described in detail the consequences of extended and vague public abstractions. Each knew of the impossibility of political community in a world in which men lost touch with their neighbors. Similarly, each confronted a world far larger and more diverse than his more classical predecessors—Plato and Rousseau, respectively—had seen manageable. Both men had raised the possibility of classical political education under circumstances far less than ideal. Each then has something significant to offer a world that *believes scientifically* that anything is possible, and *knows morally* that nothing can be achieved. De Tocqueville's prophecy offers some explanation of the source of our present discontents. Augustine's philosophical framework suggests the dangers of analytical categories that lead people either to false optimism or to false pessimism. Self-delusion of this sort was, he argued, responsible for much of fifth-century Rome's discontent.

Augustine's effort was to confront "the world of men and of time" with the power of a new idea. It was less an attempt to judge that world than it was to teach others how to begin to judge it for themselves. He placed himself in the middle of his congregation and his students, and he daily tested himself and his teaching in that context. It is this proximity of the man and his ideas to his world and his people that makes Augustine's analysis most striking and probably most anxiety-inducing to us. His was not an effort with which the contemporary analyst—preacher or teacher, theologian or political philosopher—can be comfortable. One or another aspect of his teaching may be taken seriously by contemporary activists or theorists, but the enormity of his effort is forbidding. Augustine's attempts to resolve conflicts between thought and action and between his private and public roles starkly challenge a modern world that often separates men from their ideas and ideas from any public forum. Augustine's mission at the very least was to expose the consequences of such compartmentalization.

The Weapons of the Unarmed Prophet [18]

Augustine stood with the prophetic tradition, introducing both warnings of disaster and glimpses of hope. He confronted the shortcomings of men and institutions with psychological and philosophical insights that might help each to begin anew. He sought to preserve an old teaching for those who were able to hear it, and to open to others the possibility of hearing. His was neither a gentle nor a retiring stance. He stood as a public man in militant confrontation with a world that had systematically denied the relevance of public action. Like the prophets of old, Augustine sought to reawaken a sense of common purpose that might allow men to function in a time of crisis.

John Bright describes those prophets as men who, in the face of mass skepticism of their warnings, literally saved Israel from extinction.

> By ruthlessly demolishing false hope, by announcing the calamity as Yahweh's sovereign and righteous judgment, they gave the tragedy explanation in advance in terms of faith and thereby prevented it from destroying faith.[19]

They facilitated thereby creation of a new individual and collective commitment to an Israeli community that could endure the destruction of the old. Augustine too sought to build a new community—based on individual decision—but he found himself directly implicated in the founding of that new order in a way that the prophets had not. He was at once a leader, a teacher of leaders and a teacher of citizens. He prophesied both hope and despair as had the Old Testament prophets, but in his own way. The fall of Rome was not, for Augustine, an indication of God's wrath. The birth of Christ had changed the context of secular history. A new sort of action in the world now had to be contemplated.

New leaders were needed to replace those who had absorbed classical standards and modelled their behavior on ancient heroes.[20] Also needed, however, were new principles of leadership through which those standards could be called into question. Men needed a new insight into the meaning of history. This was the new prophetic task. It was not enough to become a staff intellectual—an adviser to the bureaucratic governing class. New leaders would have to be trained, and citizens would have to be prepared to accept these new leaders and standards.

He had first sensed the need for such new categories as a teacher in Carthage, Rome, and Milan. He sought as a theologian and a bishop, as a teacher and a leader, to develop them and implement them. His successes in the *saeculum* were limited, but then so were his expectations. The power of his analysis and the nature of his insight remain. The "union of private and public interest," to which de Tocqueville looked as an antidote to both the frenzy and the withdrawal characteristic of times of crisis, was sought by Augustine as well. His public confession did not offer a set of easy answers, but then to have done so would have been in Augustine's words to invite "man's sloth" and to block potential escape from his entanglements by any "energetic pursuit of virtue." [21]

He pursued virtue and the teaching of virtue. He attempted to define the range of human character to which such teaching must be directed. He insisted that human character was such that the victories of virtue were few, but that they might come anywhere. It was necessary then that the average man become the object of his teaching. His efforts at revitalizing community demanded an attention to the particular and a breadth of vision of which the classical rhetor was incapable. The pursuit of human dignity, and the brotherhood of the community needed to support it, could not be founded solely on a narrow, classically educated elite. The earthly peace must be made to "minister to the heavenly peace," [22] Augustine insisted. This was a matter of faith to him. The "life of the city is certainly a social life," [23] he proclaimed. There were many men who could, indeed had to, support that social life. This they could do through their own righteous judgment—judgment that Augustine made the aim of his teaching.

The Confessional Teaching

In his struggle to allay private and public ills, Augustine offered what one commentator has called a therapy of self-examination.[24] Using himself as a model, Augustine presented a Socratic lesson, often strikingly modern in its psychological insights, that he hoped would foster the growth of "new men." [25] Not reliant on a catalogue of evils nor in need of a checklist against which to grade their lives, they would be able to act with an understanding of the roots of their present discontents and so, he hoped, with a clearer vision of the possible results of their present actions.

His point of departure was his own life—not as a unique example of one who had escaped the tensions and contradictions of the later antique world, but as one who confronted that world and those tensions and had found it impossible to escape.

The seductive draw of pagan success lured him into the schools of Roman rhetors and offered him a clear vantage point of the classical residue that was the public life of Roman North Africa in the late fourth century. He learned his lessons well and soon entered that arena as a teacher. His triumphs were such that he could even consider "a provincial governorship and an alliance with the local [Milanese] nobility as the next step in his career." [26] There was, however, something missing. His work was not as fulfilling as he had hoped. If the classics had answers to the pressing political, social, and psychological problems of the day, they seemed to Augustine not to be manifest in Roman public life.

There was an alternative route to public acclaim available to Augustine through the church. His mother had urged Christianity upon him in his youth, but her urging had produced only confusion and resentment. What could this alien religious belief add to his education? How could it contribute to his life and ambitions in this world? These questions were left unconfronted until Augustine sampled Roman education and public life and found them wanting. Roman praxis had faded, and Augustine—with the help of the Bishop of Milan, St. Ambrose—began to see in the Christian church a new "way of living in the world." [27] His conversion was by no means easy or rapid, but he had discovered that he could no longer ignore the tension, resentment, and emptiness that had come to dominate his life.

Augustine's confrontation with himself was a confrontation with an entire milieu—political, cultural, and religious. The tension that he felt as a result of his parents' divergent ambitions for him was a peculiarly heightened example of tension that governed the lives of many of his friends and associates.[28] He had come to know better than most of the need for new directions in leadership and new modes of confronting tension and coping with anxiety. Men would tolerate insecurity only so long, and then—as he knew from his own experience with the Manicheans—they would seek a way out. He sought more than a simple alternative to the habit and ritual of Roman public life.

Augustine's conversion was not a turn to otherworldly concerns, but a confrontation with the innerworldly demands of his own psyche. The Platonic revival, initiated by Plotinus and Porphyry, had been very important to Augustine's conversion. He began to unlock some of the mysteries of the tormented soul of his young adulthood through following Plotinus' advice to turn inward. These mysteries had not, however, been unlocked only to remain shrouded—inaccessible to all but the initiated. On the contrary, it was to those uninitiated in the complexities of classical philosophy that Augustine directed his attention. Even as he unravelled the most profound of his personal agonies, he spoke to ordinary people—people, he felt, with whom he shared an inner confusion.

Augustine had found, as had others in their Christian-Plotinian meanderings, a sense that the individual possessed "something in himself that was infinitely valuable and yet painfully unrelated to the outside world." [29] Such a recognition was, to be sure, profoundly alienating. But, Augustine argued, alienation was the first step toward liberation. Confronting the Roman system of belief in which people could calculate their place in the world with self-satisfied certainty, Augustine had first to awaken people to the danger of self-satisfaction and the error of certainty.

His own experience had taught him to know himself better and thereby to be more aware of his limitations. This was in turn the first lesson that he taught. Much of his work—formal and informal, philosophical treatise and sermon alike—thus naturally assumes a confessional aura. Augustine's confession was never self-serving. There was always the awareness of an audience. He looked to himself so that he could better understand the source of dilemmas that he felt certain were shared by many who read and listened to his words. He tried, therefore, to make his audience a part of his speaking and writing, to involve them in his own never-ending search for self-understanding. This, he insisted, is the "fruit of my confessions." [30]

Augustine had found a hint of unity and order in the human psyche that could lead people to contend more easily with the frustration and futility that were inevitably a part of life, and that seemed especially dominant in the late fourth and early fifth centuries. If he could articulate that sense of order in his own life, then he hoped, others might be able to discover it in theirs. If they could, then perhaps they could act together with a sense of purpose and integrity. Recognizing their limitations but ready to act, men might, Augustine reasoned, rediscover the potential that had atrophied in the late Roman world. Only then could he and his audience truly share their world. His own public confession was crafted to evoke the public confessions of others.

This preoccupation with his own place in his world dominated the life of St. Augustine—his analysis of the Roman world and his actions within it. The realistic [31] compromises of the Bishop of Hippo, the often beguiling, often astonishing sense of tactics and strategy that are regularly associated with his life and work must be understood in this framework. He was, to be sure, a shrewd tactician able to adapt to disparate people and circumstances with relative ease. Much of this is attributable to his cautious, even pessimistic, expectations of human nature. He did indeed react to the darker aspects of social and political life and, as one commentator suggests, etched "a dark portrait of the human condition." [32] But the existence of such obstacles never dampened his resolve to confront human limitations. His was a doctrine for active, fighting men. He could give up hope that the future would bring enduring peace and progress, [33] but at the same time cling to the more realistic wish that men might act more easily and perhaps more justly if they had more reasonable expectations about their potential.

His instruction could not be banal, but neither could it be dogmatic or utopian. For it had ultimately to awaken a new sense of potential in his student. Augustine wanted to foster independent judgment and ultimately a new hope for Christian charity. If the standard of judgment was lost in pettifogging concern over form, or if the form of instruction proved inadequate to communicate that standard, all was lost. It made little sense to Augustine to talk of such standards in the private language of the contemplative philosopher. [34]

Whether we picture Augustine as the African bishop speaking animatedly in the middle of his congregation, as an instructor of other clergy in his monastery, as a public administrator involved in the complex social and political world of fifth-century Hippo, or even as a Christian scholar puzzling over the mysteries of the Trinity, we discover a man who constantly refers back to himself—checking himself, aware of his own limitations, remembering his own struggles, and using them to instruct others. The realism of an often harsh man becomes comprehensible only when the harshness of his life and the world in which he lived are kept clearly in view.[35] His pleas as a Christian bishop for charity and justice can be understood only if they are recognized as an effort to provide an antidote to the most debilitating effects of the tensions he and his parishioners faced so regularly.

The Historical Teaching

Augustine's own judgment of Roman history—its politics and its religion—resulted from intense introspection. Thus, his more explicitly political comments in the *City of God* were as personal as the psychological and religious insights of his *Confessions.* They too breathe a confessional spirit that shapes his criticism and guides his advice throughout. He attacked Roman institutions with a sense of personal betrayal. He had been a victim of the thin veneer that was late Classical civilization. He had been taken in by the illusion of grandeur, the symbols and abstractions of empire that only pretended to serve a people.[36] He was determined to expose the fraud, so others might not have to face his disillusionment.

This situation had been the cause of many a personal tragedy, as Augustine well knew, but there was in addition a greater public malady to be confronted. Having suggested a therapy of self-examination in the first case, Augustine turned, in the *City of God,* to the development of a kind of political therapy to deal with the second. The examples of tactics and strategy that were so important to Augustine's teaching were again predominant, but had an even broader scope. All of his earlier teaching retained its significance, but now, as a foundation for further study, he turned to the examination of the history of a people. Much as Augustine had searched his memory for the details of his own existence and the cause of his misery, he would now search the memory of a civilization in an effort to better understand the source of its discontents.

The *City of God* was an edifying work, though on a level very different from that of his *Confessions.* It too was aimed carefully at an audience, but this was a different audience, a broader one. Begun after Alaric's sack of Rome in 410 A.D., it confronted in more explicit terms the decay of Rome and the social, political, and psychological disarray that grew out of it. Here, as in the *Confessions,* he attempted to pull his audience into his analysis, urging them to recognize that history was a vital part of their present existence. It was a broader teaching than the *Confessions* and in some ways necessarily more subtle. It attempted to place the individual psyche in the perspective of the history and culture of an entire people.

The human psyche was for Augustine the creation of God, and he spoke in his *Confessions* of the need to avail oneself of His healing powers. Human social and political institutions were the creation of men. His examination of the ills of these institutions and his discussion of possible remedies for those ills had, then, to be expanded to include an analysis of the founders of those institutions. In fact, one of the primary foci of the *City of God* was the study of the nature of social and political leadership.

The *City of God* was a public confession on a much grander scale than that he had offered earlier in his life, but the basic lessons were remarkably similar. Each attempted to reeducate those who would listen to the basic facts of public life and to the intensely personal and demanding nature of the commitment all must make—leader and follower alike—to the process of civic education.

The social, political, and psychological insights of his *Confessions* remained fundamental, but were now applied to an analysis of the responsibilities that leaders had to their followers.

The world shrank rapidly after 410 A.D., and Augustine quickly realized the dangers of additional dislocation, confusion, and anxiety. Men had more than ever to learn to adapt to rapidly changing circumstances, even to entirely new settings. Rome, he thought, could not provide proper guidance or leadership. He sought in the *City of God* to dissuade those who clung to Rome, to immerse them in their own history in such a way that they would understand the source of its decay. He spoke likewise to those not so persuaded by Rome but in need of an alternative. He skillfully crafted a critique of Roman political life for both groups attacking it, not as representative of classical politics but as a bastardization of it. In fact, he attacked antipolitics. And while the double negative did not produce a clearly defined positive alternative, it did seek to prepare the way for the creation of an alternative.

For all of his pessimism about the history of Rome, Augustine was concerned to illuminate principles of leadership in a practicable way.

He spoke of the limitations of human beings, especially Romans. He spoke also of human potential and of men who had accomplished some of the ideals of human association that the Romans had always claimed to seek. There were other founders, other kings, and other heroes, prophets, and teachers that should be consulted. They could be found in the Old Testament, and Augustine looked to them with great seriousness and care. He compared and contrasted the history and the politics of the Old Testament with those of Rome. He highlighted the significance of different foundations and most crucially discussed the nature of leadership that grew out of them. He was convinced that a society's founding experience was crucial to its entire existence, and that any leader concerned with maintaining basic unity and harmony had constantly to be aware of and refer to that event that had formed his particular people.

Perhaps true unity and harmony could never be found, but that made constant attention to the reaffirmation and renewal of social and political bonds all the more important. Augustine found in the scriptures an array of leaders and principles of leadership that opened to him the possibility of a significant alternative to those of Rome. Having established the possibility of such an alternative, he set about discussing its feasibility in late Roman North Africa and developing the principles of leadership most appropriate to its survival.

Augustine presented a theory of political education that, though it culminated in a careful theory of leadership in the *City of God*, was the product of many years of intellectual probing and public activity. He had introduced the tasks of the leader as political educator in his *Confessions*, and would spend many years refining them. Our task in what follows is to chart the growth of his theory of leadership—its roots in more personal writings (Part I), its development in the course of his career as a teacher and preacher (Part II), and its elaboration in the philosophical and psychological maturity of the final books of the *City of God* (Part III). From its beginning, it was a theory directed at understanding and confronting the tensions of the late antique world with the force of public confession. Subtly combining the creative potential of the classics with the everyday experience of Roman North Africa, Augustine hoped to capture some of that dialectical harmony between ancient and well-rooted principle and rapid and uprooting change that had long been the dream of statesmen and philosophers alike.

Notes

1. Peter Brown, *The World of Late Antiquity*, Harcourt Brace Jovanovich, London, 1971, p. 89. (Hereafter cited as *Late Antiquity.*)

2. Peter Brown, *Augustine of Hippo*, University of California Press, Berkeley, 1969, p. 195. (Hereafter cited as *Hippo.)*
3. F. Van der Meer, *Augustine the Bishop*, Sheed & Ward, London, 1961, pp. 259ff. (Hereafter cited as *Meer.)*
4. *Late Antiquity*, p. 93.
5. Ibid.
6. Ibid., p. 53.
7. See, for example, Eugene Kevane, "Augustine's Christian Paideia," in *Augustinian Studies*, Annual Publication of the Augustinian Institute, Villanova University, vol. I, 1970, pp. 164ff. Kevane argues persuasively that Augustine adapts Platonism to his particular audience.
8. The critical influence of Cicero, Plotinus, and others must, of course, be acknowledged. The purpose of the present work is, however, to examine the ways Augustine's synthesis of Christian and classical teachings attempted to reshape many of the most basic beliefs and commonly accepted traditions of fourth- and fifth-century Roman North Africa.
9. *Late Antiquity*, p. 131.
10. Ibid., p. 60.
11. *De Doctrina Christiana*, I, 28, J.P. Migne, vol. 34, p. 30. (Hereafter cited as *DDC.)* This is a theme that becomes more and more clear over time, as Augustine recognizes ever more clearly the dilemmas of his people in North Africa.
12. *A Select Library of the Nicene and Post-Nicene Fathers*, W.B. Eerdmans Publishing Company, Grand Rapids, Michigan, 1956, Ep. 91, vol. I, pp. 376–80. (Hereafter cited as *Epistles.)*
13. *DDC*, Migne, vol. 34, II, 25–39, pp. 55–62. *See also* Robert Marcus, *Saeculum: History and Society in the Theology of St. Augustine*, Cambridge University Press, Cambridge, 1970, pp. 96ff. (Hereafter cited as *Saeculum.)*
14. Ibid.
15. *DDC*, XIX, 17.
16. Alexis de Tocqueville, *Democracy in America*, Vintage Books, Random House, New York, 1945, vol. I, p. 252.
17. Ibid.
18. Augustine demonstrates the force of the weapons available to the man Machiavelli labelled the "unarmed prophet." Though sometimes compared to Machiavelli because of his political realism, Augustine in fact offers a powerful alternative to Machiavellian civic education.
19. John Bright, *A History of Israel*, The Westminster Press, Philadelphia, 1952, p. 317.
20. *Late Antiquity*, p. 32.
21. *The City of God Against the Pagans*, 7 vols., The Loeb Classical Library, Harvard University Press, Cambridge, Massachusetts, 1968–1972, I, 34. (Hereafter cited as *DCD.)*
22. *DCD*, XIX, 17.
23. Ibid.
24. *Hippo*, p. 181.
25. Augustine had discussed this notion of the creation of new men as early as 389 A.D. in *De vera religione*. His notion became more concrete as he became more involved with his own congregation and its day-to-day problems.

26. *Late Antiquity,* p. 30.
27. Ibid., p. 65.
28. Charles Norris Cochrane, *Christianity and Classical Culture,* Oxford-Galaxy, New York, 1957, p. 58. (Hereafter cited as *Cochrane.)*
29. *Late Antiquity,* p. 51.
30. *St. Augustine's Confessions,* 2 vols., The Loeb Classical Library, 1912, Book X. (Hereafter cited as *Confs.)*
31. See, for example, Herbert A. Deane, *The Social and Political Ideas of St. Augustine,* Columbia University Press, New York, 1966.
32. Ibid., p. 241.
33. Ibid, p. 243.
34. Augustine had flirted with the contemplative life immediately after his conversion, but was active in Hippo by the time he wrote his *Confessions.*
35. *Hippo.*
36. For a discussion of Augustine's definition of a people and his comments on Cicero, see *DCD,* II, 21, and XIX, pp. 21, 24.

CHAPTER 1

The Confessional Method
of a Public Man:
An Introduction to the *Confessions*

This is the fruit of my Confessions, not of what I have been, but of what I am; namely to confess this not only before Thee only, in a secret rejoicing mixed with trembling, and in a hidden grief allayed with hope: but in the ears also of the believing sons of men, sharers of my joy, and partners in mortality with me; my fellow citizens and my fellow pilgrims. . . .

Confessions, X, 4

In a number of ways, the *Confessions* endures as the heart of St. Augustine's writings. It is not only the philosophical center of his work, but more importantly, it is a surprisingly personal attempt to create a political philosophy that emanates from a searching and anxious soul. The emotionality of the *Confessions* introduces a man struggling to find the strength to face a chaotic world, while at the same time trying to influence the shape of that world. Its structural intricacies present a work in which the mysterious is united with the commonplace—the most private of thoughts with the public world of the Coloseum. What begins as an examination of his own life quickly becomes as well an examination of the lives of others and of the social, political, and cultural milieus which they shared.

Augustine begins his *Confessions* with a discussion of his youth. He knew that the education of the young was critical to the development

15

of energetic and virtuous citizens. Roman civic education had not contributed much to the life of the young Augustine, and he saw that many others had been miseducated as well. He sets out, therefore, in the narrative of his *Confessions* to discover an alternative to the Roman educational system [1] that he can offer to the people of Roman North Africa.

Always conscious of the inadequacies of his own upbringing, and keenly aware of the importance of the lessons and examples of good teachers, Augustine became a teacher. His teaching, as suggested above, was both personal and public, and is probably best characterized as public confession. It was public in its sensitivity to the life experiences of others and in its call for common action for the good of all. It was confessional both in its reflection of his own experiences and as a praise of God. The *Confessions* demonstrates some of Augustine's greatest skills as a teacher, presenting the most complex material in personal and emotional terms accessible to ordinary people—the most mysterious and probing of questions in a public, instructive, educative mode. In all of these ways, the *Confessions* set the tone for much that followed.

One should begin reading the *Confessions* with an image of Augustine pacing back and forth in his monastery in Hippo, dictating a treatise that he hoped would touch the passions, fears, and hopes of his audience. His picture of that audience was alive and detailed. A friend who needed encouraging, an enemy who warranted attacking, a parishioner who needed prodding—each felt the carefully pointed words of the bishop. Augustine found his way into the heart of every man.[2] After despairing of man's condition, he would offer a glimmer of hope but pull back at the last minute lest that hope turn to the arrogance of pride. Here as always, Augustine was a part of the world in which he lived. Pace though he might in the confines of his monastery, he confronted Hippo, Carthage, and Roman North Africa with nearly daily sermons to the people.

He was involved in the people's lives during this period, as he would be for the rest of his days.[3] We must, one writer suggests, participate with Augustine in the formulation of his questions.[4] The pacing then becomes intense; the men he addresses become real; the task in which he engaged becomes immense. Augustine sought to weave words and emotions in a fashion that reminds one of Wittgenstein's *Philosophical Investigations:*

> If language is to be a means of communication there must be agreement not only in definitions but also (queer as this may sound) in judgments. This seems to abolish logic but does not do so.[5]

Augustine questioned the judgment of his audience and was confronted by lack of agreement on many levels. His *Confessions* was his attempt to seek out and tap common feeling of both despair and hope. Only then could he build those latent common feelings into a new foundation—the basis, he hoped, for common judgment—judgment that might reshape their lives.

Three general themes emerge from these early sections of the *Confessions.* Central, of course, is the public-private dilemma already outlined. But two related issues must also be discussed. First, Augustine's description of the development of a healthy individual as the basis of a renewed society is critical, for it allows us to specify his diagnosis of the ills of Roman society. Second, his development of a mode of instruction through public confession introduces us to his treatment of these same ills. Each of these three themes warrants careful consideration.

The Private Purposes of a Public Order

St. Augustine—even in the inner depths of his private contemplation—retained the consciousness of a public man. That consciousness could become a nuisance, but it was one that his sense of responsibility taught him he should not avoid. Augustine was well aware of the conflict between the public order and private interests. He confronted that conflict with a recognition that it could never be fully resolved, yet he never ceased working toward such a resolution. The problem is a complex one—familiar to the history of Western political thought. It is, in Augustine's terms, a four-fold problem that might be expressed as follows:

	Roman	Augustinian
Private	Atomized Estranged (Alienatio)	Self-awareness
Public	Rote, Custom and Habit	Christian Charity and fraternity

The mix of public and private worlds was, for Augustine, inevitable. Even in a Roman setting where individuals indulged themselves with little regard for public consequences, private actions shaped the character of the public world.

These individuals were estranged[6] from their fellows. Interaction came only in the form of rote custom and habit. The young Augustine understood that public life in turn reinforced the isolation that was the reality of the Roman world. The only cure for the public disease that he had discovered festering in Hippo in the mid-390s was an attack on the consciousness of a public mind that he thought to be semiconscious at best. Again, public and private concerns were combined. The only way to introduce people to the hope of Christian charity and fraternity was through making them conscious of the limitations, the dangers, and the fears that dominated their private lives.

The *Confessions* thus introduces a dialogue between the private and public spheres of existence that works toward a resolution of conflict based on the fact that God's "truth is neither mine, nor his, nor another's; but belongs to us all, when Thou publicly callest to have it in common, warning us terribly not to account it private to ourselves for fear we be deprived of it."[7]

Individual and Society

Augustine thought that each individual passes through several stages of development on his way to maturity. The capacity to make and sustain judgments about oneself and one's society grew only after careful earlier training. He worried that the experiences in his own infancy, childhood, and adolescence had impeded his development as an independent young man. The customs in the midst of which he was cast as a boy encouraged, he tells us, a dependence on the superficial whims of fickle crowds.[8] Success, as a person, depended upon eloquence. Augustine's masters in turn seemed less concerned with him as a person than with the good repute that his success might bring to them. Thus his sense of himself was tainted, and he was in a poor position to offer anything of value either to his fellows or to the society at large. This early training or lack thereof could, he feared, have a grave impact on future social and political questions. Indeed, he notes that the sins and games of the young often prompted and encouraged by their elders are directly

> transferred from governors and masters, from nuts, and balls, and sparrows, to magistrates and kings, to gold and lands, and slaves, just as the rod is succeeded by more severe chastisements.[9]

The early stages of individual development are, he insists, critical to the healthy growth of whole societies as well as individuals.

An individual who lacks self-confidence and is unable to assess the virtue of a particular leader or policy will, Augustine felt, make a poor citizen. His loyalty will be shallow and transient, his susceptibility to despotism constant. A political society composed of such citizens will be in constant danger of fragmentation. Rome, suggested Augustine, is and has been such a society.

Much later in the *City of God*, he will note the importance of the diagnosis of individual weaknesses and strengths as preliminary to any study of society "since each individual is to the republic or kingdom what one letter is to a whole discourse, namely the elementary particle." [10] In the *Confessions*, he lays the foundation for that further analysis. Later he will note that "the true education of the human race . . . was like that of an individual. It advances by steps in time, as the individual's does when a new stage of life is reached." [11] In the *Confessions*, he focuses on the enslavement of the individual both in his own body and by the opinion of the mob. He hopes that diagnosis on the individual level will make larger social and political diagnoses more fruitful. He is certain that the treatment of those larger social and political diseases must begin with the individual.

If indeed "the happiness of a city and the happiness of an individual human being" are the same,[12] then it is incumbent upon Augustine first to discover the source of the happiness of an individual. This quest is central to his *Confessions*. Unhappiness, he suggests, looking to his own miserable youth, was the result of weakness that prohibited him from developing self-confidence. Seemingly unable to do anything without the approval of masters, parents, or friends, he was constantly at war with himself. It was as though he were an actor playing many roles, his very identity as a person depending upon his fellow players and/or the audience that observed his plays and games. Augustine battled those carnal customs [13] that had blocked the spiritual and so made him "unwilling to exercise self-scrutiny. . . ." [14] His will seemed to him to lack power—a phenomenon undoubtedly familiar to his readers. He continued to search for a position where "to will was to do. . . ." [15] This fruitful combination of willing and doing constituted the happiness of the individual. A number of such individuals brought together would, he reasoned, create a healthy and happy society.

Mad that he might be whole and free and happy,[16] Augustine battles with himself in the *Confessions* to the point of his conversion. This was the source of his new happiness. His "free will [was] called forth in a moment," he says, "Whereby I submitted to Thy easy yoke. . . . How pleasant did it suddenly become to me to be without the delights of trifles!" [17] His relief and praise were directed at a captivated audience.

Attention was drawn away from Christian mystery and turned to a general sense of relief, so that at least some of the burdens of Augustine's troubled youth had been lifted. Now he could begin to describe—by way of contrast as well as relief—the new state of his mind and the freedom he had found. His new personality depended on the possibility of self-examination and the beginning of self-identification. It was not a freedom that eliminated all dependence, but one that flourished under a new variety of dependence within the structure of God's love. It was, he says, an "easeful liberty." [18] It had granted no easy answers, but had made the search for them more manageable for Augustine and so, he hoped, for his readers as well.

Augustine remained self-scrutinizing and continued his search for God.[19] His conversion was merely a prolegomenon and offered no final answers. It gave free curiosity the creative playground it needs.

> Now was my soul free from the gnawing cares of seeking and getting, and of wallowing and exciting the itch of lust. And I babbled unto Thee my brightness, my riches and my health, the Lord my God.[20]

This new found health—physical and mental—had not, to be sure, totally exempted him from pain. Still troubled by temptation, Augustine found the power of his dreams difficult to tolerate. It was a reminder of the basic conflict between his awakening search for *caritas* and the reality of the lust still in his soul.[21] He had not been freed from his body, as the Lord reminded him, with a toothache.[22] He would have to seek health not only within his soul and body but within a community of souls and bodies who shared his longings. He had been freed to search for a new way of life, but within strict limits. This was all that was possible, but under the circumstances it was a great deal.

Augustine began to deal with that world that had by its habits and custom so limited him. His was not an escape from the world but a start at living more freely within it. It was not an escape from other people but a new understanding of the foundations of personal relationships. To know oneself was to be open to charity *(caritas)*.

His *Confessions* thus declares its purpose in a search for the brotherly mind—the fraternal soul that directs Augustine to serve his brethren. The call is finally explicit! He turns away from a concern with autobiographical detail—though that detail remains in the memory of the reader. What had begun as a withdrawal from the world emerges as a new involvement in it. The *Confessions* becomes an indication of that involvement, and at the same time a kind of test of it. A. Solignac suggests, for example, that in the presence of God all men actively confess. The *Confessions*, he argues, promotes that activity, presenting itself "as a work for the community of all faithful Christians, as a fraternal testimony which must serve all. . . ." [23]

The wholeness that Augustine had sought and continued to seek was more than that of a psychological harmony. He sought an attachment to *(diligo)* and a continuing strong relationship *(caritas)* with other people. The sense that his readers matter to him is pervasive. In fact, it becomes clear that they must play a part in his becoming whole. Augustine's strength and independence as an individual was directly involved in his relationship with his reader. He suggests, in fact, at the conclusion of the autobiographical section of his *Confessions*, that it is his readers' response that is most crucial to him. He asks that all who "shall read these Confessions" be mindful of the transitory nature of this life and learn, through a study of the trials and tribulations of his life and the life of his parents, to better understand themselves and one another. [24]

Public Instruction Through Public Confession

Augustine's public confessions were intended to foster self-observation, the first step toward a new public position. One is given the suggestion of a way to escape madness, [25] to reveal secret, hidden places, [26] and to face the world with a new and "easeful" liberty.

The confessional style is an integral part of this inward-looking process. The reader is led through it to see and think about Augustine as he was, confessing the sins of his past—*confessio peccati,* and Augustine as he is, freely praising God—*confessio laudem.* [27] This process was also intended to stimulate an analysis of himself, i.e., the reader, as he is and as he might be. This was his expressed object, even in the face of obvious criticism: "Let . . . the strong and mighty laugh at me," he said, "but let us weak and needy souls ever confess unto Thee." [28] He offered strength to act in a world in which public action has been stifled, but he insisted that it came only with that self-understanding that exposed unconscious dependencies.

This confession of praise, which, says Augustine, brings people close to God and offers them a new kind of freedom, must be preceded by a clear recognition of the difficulties of this life. [29] Through his example, Augustine sought to encourage his readers to face their own weakness, and hence to appreciate their potential strength.

> This is the fruit of my Confessions, not of what I have been, but of what I am; namely to confess this not before Thee only, in a secret rejoic-

ing mixed with trembling, and in a hidden grief allayed with hope: but in the ears also of the believing sons of men, sharers of my joy, and partners in mortality with me; my fellow citizens and my fellow pilgrims. . . .[30]

Augustine's life had changed radically since his days in Milan as a teacher of classical rhetoric. Rejecting the selling of technique in the "market place of loquacity,"[31] he became a moral educator. That change was always (for him) one that implicated others—others for whom he felt responsibility. Well trained in classical public skills, Augustine's ability as a preacher was considerable. It permitted him a special kind of access to a wide variety of audiences. He maintained a personal sensitivity, an awareness of audience that was truly remarkable.[32] He never stopped projecting himself into his work. His own experiences informed his responses to the most complicated questions of philosophy or Christian doctrine [33] and to the most simple of everyday occurrences.[34]

That the circumstances he had endured and the life he had found had relevance for many others in North Africa was also clear to him. Finding a common and ordinary existence among fellow sufferers was all that he could ask. Roman praxis had made such a search difficult. The decay of Roman praxis now made it necessary. He hoped to pass on some of the lessons that he had learned—to short circuit some of the difficulties and to make what was at best a painful existence less so.

The *Confessions* as a statement of his own weakness and pain—*confessio peccati*—and of his praise of God—*confessio laudis*—states the basic premises of a very personal position and begins that hard work of Christian instruction. Men often misunderstand the meaning of praise, he suggested. They seek to strengthen themselves through the opinion that other people have of them only to discover that they have become imprisoned by that opinion. "This madness put far from me, O Lord," he prays, "lest my own mouth prove the oil of sinners unto me, to make fat my head." [35] Augustine knew the difficulty of escaping the bondage of opinion and custom. He had, as well, reason to understand more clearly the purity of praise—i.e., praise given, not praise received—and to attempt to praise the source of his own release from that bondage. He hoped that he could, through his praise, instruct others in the ways of a strength that was independent of custom and opinion.[36]

Thus the *Confessions,* though it formed a bare beginning to the work of Christian instruction, sets a tone in style and in substance for much that follows. In its sensitivity to a potentially diverse audience, it is still beyond compare. In its simultaneous confrontation with religious, political, and psychological issues of great complexity, it sought to reach many facets of its diverse audience and offered each one a path to self-understanding.

Memoria, Caritas, *and Christian Community*

Augustine's dramatic example could awaken curiosity, but that awakening was not in itself sufficient. His readers would have to do more than follow Augustine's lead, if they were to repeat the job of self-analysis that Augustine had asked them to begin. As soon as each remembered the details of his own past and came to recognize the unconscious hold of that past—its unquestioned mores, customs, and rituals—he had then to become conscious of the process of memory itself.

His autobiographical comments had gained him the attention of his audience. He had then to teach them to examine themselves. He begins the task in earnest in Book X of the *Confessions* in a discussion of memory, continues with a discussion of the nature of time—and human action with time—in Book XI and concludes with an introduction to the reading of the scriptures. The point of departure for his more spiritual or philosophic teaching is, not surprisingly, an analysis of memory. That place, he says, where "I meet with myself": [37]

> There [in my memory] are all which I remember, either by personal experience or on the faith of others. Out of the same supply do I myself with the past construct now this, now that likeness of things, which either I have experienced, or, from having experienced, have believed; and thence again future actions, events and hopes, and upon all these again do I meditate as if they were present. "I will do this or that," I say to myself in that vast womb of my mind, filled with the images of things so many and so great, "and this or that shall follow upon it." "Oh that this or that might come to pass!" "God avert this or that!" Thus I speak to myself, out of the same treasury of memory; nor could I say anything at all about them were the images absent.[38]

This is no mechanical process either. *Memoria* is an enormous and broadly inclusive concept.

> Behold, in those innumerable fields, and dens, and caves of my memory, innumerably full of innumerable kinds of things, brought in, first, either by the images, as all bodies are; secondly, or by the presence of the things themselves, as the arts are; thirdly, or by certain notions or impressions, as the affections of the mind are,—which even then when the mind doth suffer, yet doth the memory retain, since whatsoever is in the mind, is also in the memory:—through all these do I run and fit about, on this side, and on that side, mining into them so far as ever I am able,

> but can find no bottom. So great is the force of memory, so great is the force of life, even in man living as mortal.[39]

Coming to terms with one's memory was then coming to terms with oneself. It is the recognition of those "secret caverns" of the mind that hide within them the secrets of the past that need to be called forth. It represents a confrontation with the distracting passions [40]—desire, joy, fear, and sorrow. Self-analysis required more than mechanical problem-solving.[41] In the end it is "I myself" that I seek. After having discovered himself, and only then, he could pass beyond memory and finally escape the crippling bonds of Roman custom.

A true understanding of the self required an ongoing process of confrontation with forces that attempted constantly to interfere with self-perception. These forces came both from within in the form of dreams and unconscious yearnings and from without in the form of a culture that denied the significance of the sort of self-examination that Augustine advocated. The proper use of memory would, he hoped, facilitate that process of self-examination, and it would lead to spiritual renewal that would in turn promote a new individual and collective commitment to justice and new action in support of that commitment.

The Teachings of Scripture

The word of the scripture and the example of Christ would in the end provide the most central educational devices. But Augustine knew from personal experience of the difficulties that the uninitiated faced in reading the scriptures and of the intense and complex demands that Christian piety imposed.[42] Individuals had to be prepared for such instruction. Augustine saw this as the mediating task of the first ten books of his *Confessions*. He could then turn to the more difficult problems of scriptural interpretation in the last three books, as he instructs his reader in an introduction to the book of Genesis.

God's law was an instrument of instruction. It provided an authoritative guide to the free curiosity of youth and an instructional counsel to the despair of their elders.

> Thy laws, O God, yes, thy laws, even from the schoolmaster's ferule, to the martyr's trials, being able to temper wholesome and bitter together, calling us back by that means unto thyself, even from that infectious sweetness, which first allured us to fall away from thee.[43]

There was a specific place to look. The message of the scripture might not always be readily apparent, but there was there a starting point—of this his reader was assured.

Augustine himself had had great difficulty with the scriptures at first. In fact he described them as unworthy, in comparison to the classical texts he had read.[44] Even after his conversion, he reports that he had difficulty with Isaiah.[45] To reach the point where one could truly delight in the law was difficult, he knew, and even then its message could be clouded. Nonetheless, he seeks to reassure his readers, reminding them that even after his conversion, "I delight in the law of God, in my inmost self, but I see in my members another law at war with the law of my mind and making me captive to the law of sin which dwells in my members." [46] His task was to instruct himself—and his reader—in the law of the scriptures so the law of the flesh could more regularly be brought under control.

Ambrose had taught Augustine that there was no mechanical formula available to one who sought to understand the law. Augustine in turn spoke of the way in which he slowly grew to appreciate more fully the content of the scriptures, remembering always Ambrose's admonition to his parishioners that the "letter killeth and Spirit giveth life."

> I rejoiced . . . that the old Scripture of the law and the prophets were laid before me, to be perused, not now with that eye to which they seemed most absurd before, when I censured Thy holy ones for so thinking, when as in truth they thought not so; and with delight I heard Ambrose, in his sermons to the people, oftentimes most diligently recommend this text as a rule—The letter killeth but the spirit giveth life," while, *drawing aside the mystic veil,* he spiritually laid open that which accepted according to the letter, seemed to teach perverse doctrines—teaching herein nothing that offended me, though he taught such things as I knew not as yet whether they were true.[47]

The gentleness of Ambrose as an instructor combined with his message to provide Augustine with a foundation to which he would constantly refer from that time on. Like his teacher, he was unwilling to enter into technical disputes about the meaning of specific passages and words, "for that is profitable to nothing but to the subverting of hearers," he said. "But the law is good to edify, if man use it lawfully; [that is] for the end of charity out of a pure heart, and a good conscience and a faith un-feigned." [48] The law could be used to teach the people, he argued, but only if all who sought its truth "love one another, and equally love Thee, our God. . . ." [49] Augustine's goal was the same as was Paul's, "to teach and show unto us a more excellent way to charity." [50] Augustine believed that people would not always respond to reasoned argument or to a patient rendering of God's law and its value. In addition to that rendering, therefore, Augustine had to maintain the openness of Ambrose, as he faced the diversity and conflict of fourth-century Roman North Africa.

Augustine's understanding of his teacher's wise words is made clear in Book XII of the *Confessions,* as he speaks of Moses and prays, had he been enjoined to write the book of Genesis,

> that such power of expression and such a method of arrangement should be given me, that they who cannot as yet understand how God creates might not reject the words as surpassing their powers; and they who are already able to do this, would find, in what true opinion so ever they had by thought arrived at, that it was not passed over in the few words of Thy servant; and should another man by the light of truth discover another, neither should that fail to be found in those same words.[51]

These were his goals as a teacher. The suggestion is that his own power of expression and method of arrangement were directed at a broad, diverse audience and offered, he hoped, many points of access to his ideas. His was not a secret teaching. On the contrary it could and, for him, had to be made available to the broadest audience, some of whom would in turn continue his teaching. He hoped

> that whatever truth any one might apprehend concerning these matters, my words should re-echo, rather than that I should set down one true opinion so clearly on his as that I should exclude the rest.[52]

The scriptures are and would remain, he argued, a message to the people. They reach out to each in his own circumstances. His hope is that his writing can accomplish the same through an understanding of

> the natural man, like him who is a babe in Christ, and a sucker of milk, till such time as he grows big enough for strong meat. . . ."[53]

That natural man could be reached and made to feel contented. Augustine hoped through his *Confessions* to provide such contentment by granting access to God's law. They might *then* pursue a life that reflects the commandments of scripture and discover an alternative to the bankrupt moral order against which Augustine stood in dramatic confrontation. They might as well truly learn something of the significance of Christ's example.

Christ as Mediator

"To cure man's *superbia*," Augustine argues, "God's son descended and became humble."[54] Christ's love was at once an antidote to pride and an example for men to follow. Indeed, his humility and his charity were necessary precursors to effective self-examination. The failure of Roman "civil theology"[55] suggested the failure of a belief system that followed prideful custom rather than truth. Augustine sought a religion that would directly promote fellowship—human and angelic. God's grace, manifested in Christ's love, promoted activity truly worthy of men. Men were dependent on the authority of Christ, but Christ in turn offered men the hope of *caritas*—mutual affection and concern— that made that authority not just bearable but liberating.

The new common strength and hope offered through *caritas* provided the impetus for realistic confrontation with the problems of day-to-day life. For Augustine, Christ thus becomes the concrete manifestation of the return to the cave. Plato too recognized the responsibility of the representatives of the truth, but—at least for Augustine—was unable to offer any real hope that those responsibilities could be met.[56] Augustine's task was to make sure that this message would be understood for what it was. It was, he insisted, a message for the common man. One that he could and so must act upon.

Thus, the role of Christ both as an example and as a mediator between God and man is crucial for Augustine. "For as a man he was Mediator; but as the Word He was not between because he was equal to God. . . ."[57] In that he was also man, he presented to man for his inspection an example that could be described in concrete terms. For people like him who had doubt or were absorbed in mystery, Christ's very humanity was the key. Developed throughout his *Confessions,* this theme is summarized by Augustine in a 412 A.D. letter.

> *Instruction* came by Him, because those truths which had been, for men's advantage, spoken before that time on earth not only by the holy prophets, all whose words were true, but also by philosophers and even poets and authors in every department of literature, might by the actual presentation of His authority in *human nature* be confirmed as true *for the sake of those who could not perceive and distinguish them* in the light of essential Truth. . . .[58] (emphasis added).

The wholeness that Augustine sought could not be completely attained through using Christ as an example to be imitated, but His very existence opened a series of possibilities for education of the many. "Christ," he argued, "died for all, that they should not henceforth live unto themselves. . . ."[59] Now there was available for everyone a glimpse at the perfection that Plato could discuss only with a certain few. Christ's mediating role was then even more profound than that of the philosopher-king. He offered instruction in justice, and as such, became a substitute for the "noble lie." Augustine's task in his *Confes-*

sions was to make Christ's humble example known and available to Everyman.

Once Christ's humble example was introduced, it was possible, Augustine felt, for people to begin to understand themselves in new ways, not just as individuals but as members of a society who shared a vision of the "truest common good." For in Christ there was, he argued, not simply instruction for the individual but also there is

> security for the welfare and renown of a commonwealth; for no state is perfectly established and preserved otherwise than on the foundation and by the bond of faith and of firm concord, when *the highest and truest common good*, namely, God, is loved by all, and men love each other in Him without dissimulation, because they love one another for His sake from whom they cannot disguise the real character of their love. [60]

That common action in service of the highest common good must, of course, follow the success of the prior instructional task.

In sum, his educational/confessional method aimed at the creation of an Augustinian/Christian community that combined Platonic training in self-analysis with Christ's example of self-sacrifice. It sought to develop both the strength of individual freedom and self-control and to engender respect for the authority and guidance of God's grace. Two commandments summarized all for Augustine—Love God. Love your neighbor as yourself! His community depended upon the proper understanding of these two. An ordinate self-love first allowed and then encouraged proper love of one's neighbor. Ordinate self-love was only possible because of God's grace. One must, however, openly love God in order to recognize his grace and act upon it for oneself and one's neighbor.

> For this very end did he love us that we also should love one another, bestowing this on us by His own love to us, that we should be bound to one another in mutual love, and united together as members by so pleasant a bond, should be the body of so mighty a head.[61]

For Augustine, God's grace is a fact. Men's wills are not, however, always strong enough to receive it, let alone act upon it. His educational aim is to strengthen those wills in order to allow individuals to understand themselves. For then, and only then, could they understand and love others. Only then could a Christian community based on *caritas* emerge to fill the vacuum created by the failures of Roman social and political institutions.

Conclusion

The acknowledgement of understandable and accessible human problems makes Augustine's a plea to Everyman, and began the instructional task at its most elemental point—the attention of his people. "The power of the bonds of all habit," he says, "even upon a mind which now feeds not upon a fallacious word" [62] is great. This he acknowledged in his *Confessions* and elsewhere—sometimes matter of factly, sometimes emotionally, sometimes philosophically. From the common-sense response of a child to what seemed like meaningless parental oppression to more complicated problems of Roman education, Augustine attempted to make the most ordinary happenings in life the source of a new self-consciousness. He did not seek immediate converts, nor did he imply that all should follow his path in every detail. His only plea was that his reader recognize the impediments to happiness—individual and collective—imbedded in the seemingly innocent habits and customs of everyday life. "But," he says, "woe unto thee thou stream of human custom! Who shall stay thy course? How long will it be before thou driest up?" [63]

The threat Augustine felt was a real and immediate one. The fiction of classical education led men into a hell of self-deception. He described this problem in the first book of his *Confessions.*

> Yet, O hellish flood, men's sons are thrown into thee, with their tuition fees, so that they may learn these things. This is an important business, when carried on publicly in the forum, in full view of the laws governing the payment in salaries over and above fees. Thou beatest upon the stones along thy course and thy reverberations say: "Here is where words are learned; here is where eloquence is gained, most essential for persuasion and for the development of opinions." [64]

Roman teachers pretended to educate children to a public world but in fact deceived them. This custom infected the very source of society in the education of its children.

> Woe unto thee, O flood of human customs! Who will resist thee? How long will it be before thou driest up? How much further wilt thou roll the sons of Eve unto that great and fearful sea, over which those can hardly pass who embark upon the wood of the Cross?
>
> Who, among these begowned teachers, can listen undisturbed when a man from their own dust declaims, saying: "Homer invented these fictions and transferred human traits to the gods; I should prefer that divine ones be given to us." It is more truly said that he did, indeed, make up these fictions, yet thereby attributed divinity to disgraceful men, so

that their disgraces would not be regarded as such, and that whoever did likewise would seem to be imitating the gods in heaven rather than abandoned men.[65]

Learning from their teachers, children had been cast into their society with a set of public examples and standards of excellence with which, Augustine argued, could lead only to disaster.

Augustine was claiming neither that a truly public world was easily acquired, nor that all custom was inimical to such a world. He merely wanted to open for examination the actual nature of Roman custom. It was not to be judged on its own terms. In fact, he notes:

> There are some [offenses] which resemble offenses of infamy or violence, and yet are not sins because they neither offend Thee, our Lord God, nor social custom: when, for example, things suitable for the times are provided for the use of life, and we are uncertain whether it be out of lust of having; or when acts are punished by constituted authority for the sake of correction, and we are uncertain whether it be out of a lust for hurting. Many a deed, then, which in the sight of men is disapproved, is approved by Thy testimony; and many a one who is praised by men is, Thou being witness, condemned; because frequently the view of the deed, and the mind of the doer, and the hidden exigency of the period, severally vary.[66]

The problem that is set before man, argued Augustine, is to search for the standard whereby circumstances of these types are judged. People must examine their own lives with great care and recognize that custom and habit are not self-justifying or, as argued more directly, many a custom that seems to support the public order may in fact be opposed to it.

Justice was the only true standard of judgment, and people must be made to see that it is not "various and changeable." This truth is difficult to comprehend because justice presides over times that "are not alike because they are times." There were, however, matters of fact that could be observed, if one simply took the time. Indeed, through a careful process of self- and social examination, one could begin to understand what was at stake in loving the "good of all" more than "our own private good." [67]

If Christian churches were to become, as Augustine hoped that they would, "sacred seminaries of public instruction in which" the best of Roman public morality was to be revived, "inculcated and learned," [68] then it would be necessary to lay a very careful foundation. In his *Confessions,* in his sermons, in his pastoral work, and in other more formal treatises on moral education,[69] Augustine prepared the way for the restoration of a Classical public virtue that Rome had failed to sustain.[70] Augustine in these earlier works initiated a search for the causes of moral decline that he would conclude many years later in the *City of God.* In the weakness of his will and those of his fellow North Africans, he discovered the central cause. He sought a new strength in which "the power is all the one with the will; and the willing is now the doing." [71] Yet he knew as well that the mind was "slow to goodness," [72] and that much careful training would have to precede active and charitable "willing."

Perhaps it would thus be more accurate to label Augustine's thought in his *Confessions*—after the fashion of Socrates in the *Gorgias*—as prepolitical theory. In the *Gorgias,* after a long discussion of the demands of public life, Socrates reminds his students that, beyond their self-deceptions, they are "deplorably uneducated." Each must dedicate himself, he insists, to a training that must be *preliminary* to any direct involvement in politics.

> And after such training in common together, then, at last, if we think fit, we may enter public life, or we may take counsel together on whatever course suggests itself, when we are better able to take counsel than now.[73]

Notes

1. *St. Augustine's Confessions,* 2 vols., The Loeb Classical Library, 1912, Book X. *(Confs.)*
2. Robert J. O'Connell, *Saint Augustine's Confessions: The Odyssey of the Soul,* Harvard University Press, Cambridge, 1969, p. 186. (Hereafter cited as *Odyssey.)*
3. For accounts of the life and times of St. Augustine, see F. Van der Meer, *Augustine The Bishop,* Sheed & Ward, London, 1961 (Meer), and Peter Brown's *Augustine of Hippo and Religion and Society in the Age of St. Augustine,* University of California Press, Berkeley, 1962 *(Hippo).*
4. David Burrell, "Reading the Confessions: An Exercise in Theological Understanding," *Journal of Religion,* vol. 50, 1970, p. 329.
5. Ibid., p. 330.
6. See Robert Markus' "Alienatio," *Studia Patristica,* vol. IX, 1963, pp. 431–50.
7. *Confs.,* XII, 25.
8. Ibid., I, 19.
9. Ibid.
10. *The City of God Against the Pagans,* 7 vols., The Loeb Classical Library, Harvard University Press, Cambridge, Massachusetts, 1968–1972, IV, 3. *(DCD.)*
11. Ibid., X, 14.
12. Ibid., I, 15.

13. See, e.g., *Confs.* IX, 12.
14. *Confs.*, VIII, 7.
15. Ibid., VIII, 8.
16. Ibid., VII, 14.
17. Ibid., VIII, 10.
18. Ibid., IX, 3.
19. Ibid., IX, 1.
20. Ibid.
21. Ibid., X, 30.
22. *Confs.*, IX. One is reminded here of earlier pains that Augustine endured at the deathbed of a friend *(Confs.,* IV, pp. 6–7). Now the pain was more direct, and it is overcome with the help of a new kind of friendship as he and his companions pray together for relief, thereby establishing a new foundation for their relationship.
23. A. Solignac, "Introduction" to *Les Confessions,* Oeuvres St. Augustin, Traduction de E. Tré Lorel et G. Boissou, Desclée de Brower, 1962, vol. 13, pp. 17–18. (Hereafter cited as Solignac.)
24. *Confs.*, IX, 13.
25. *Confs.*, X, 37.
26. Ibid.
27. *Confs.*, I, 5. See also *Enarrationes in Psalmos, Opera omnia, Patrologiae cursus completus* . . . Series Latina, J.P. Migne, Paris, 1842, vol. 37, pp. 1774–75. (Hereafter cited as Migne.)
28. *Confs.*, IV, 1.
29. Difficulties much like those that he discusses in the first nine books of his *Confessions.*
30. *Confs.*, X, 4.
31. Ibid., IX, 2.
32. See Meer, and *Hippo.*
33. There is no clearer example of this than Augustine's discussion of memory in Book X of his *Confessions.* The experience of examining his own past has clearly led him here to a subtle and sophisticated philosophical discussion.
34. Peter Brown refers to several of these examples that are to be found throughout Augustine's letters and sermons.
35. *Confs.*, X, 38.
36. Solignac (p. 164) argues that:

> Les *Confessions* . . . ne sont pas seulement un aveu mais aussi une prédication. En les rédigeant, Augustin reste pasteur et docteur: il veut guider, il veut enseigner; il y réussit de manière très concrète à l'occasion des événements de sa propre vie et de la vie des autres personages qui interviennent dans le récit; il le fait discrètement d'ailleurs et sans appuyer sur la leçon: il lui suffit de proposer ses propres réflexions dans l'intention d'en susciter de semblables chez son lecteur.

> He is not suggesting that custom and opinion must be ignored. On the contrary, they form the basis of the world in which he and his audience live, and must be carefully accounted for and addressed with great respect. In fact, he addresses himself to this very issue in Book XII, and argues

that one must allow for many different customs. He asks only that men be
aware that those customs and opinions may work against them.

37. *Confs.*, X, 8.
38. Ibid.
39. Ibid., X, 17.
40. Ibid., X, 14.
41. Ibid., X, 16.
42. See, for example, *Confs.*, IX, 5.
43. *Confs.*, I, 14.
44. *Confs.*, III, 5.
45. *Confs.*, IX, 5.
46. *Confs.*, VII, 16.
47. *Confs.*, VI, 4.
48. *Confs.*, XII, 18.
49. *Confs.*, XII, 30.
50. Ibid.
51. *Confs.*, XII, 26.
52. *Confs.*, XII, 31.
53. *Confs.*, XIII, 18.
54. Cited in Anders Nygren, *Agape and Eros*, Philip S. Watson trans., Harper
    and Row, New York, 1969, p. 473. (Hereafter cited as Nygren.) *See also
    Confs.* II, 6, and *A Select Library of the Nicene and Post-Nicene Fathers*,
    W. B. Eerdmans Publishing Company, Grand Rapids, Michigan, 1956, Ep.
    91, vol. I, pp. 376-80.
55. *DCD*, IX, 4.
56. See, for example, *Confs.* VII, 21 and more extensive discussion of Christ's
    love in Chapter 4 below.
57. *Confs.*, X, 43.
58. *Ep.*, 137.3.12, p. 478.
59. *Confs.*, X, 43.
60. *Ep.*, 137.5.17, p. 480.
61. *In Joanis Evangelicum* LV, 2, J.P. Migne, vol. 35, p. 1787. (Hereafter cited
    as *In Jo. Ev.)*
62. *Confs.*, IX, 12.
63. Ibid.
64. Ibid., I, 16.
65. Ibid.
66. *Confs.*, III, 9.
67. *Confs.*, III, 8. The temptation to compare these insights to those of Rou-
    sseau in the *Social Contract* and in the *Second Discourse* is great, but it
    will be left for further development in Chapter 5.
68. *Ep.*, 91.3, p. 377.
69. For example, see *De Magistro, De Doctrina Christiana*, and *De Cate-
    chizandis Rudibus*, and discussion of these works in Chapter 5.
70. See, for example, *DCD*, II, 27.
71. *Confs.*, VIII, 8.
72. *Confs.*, VIII, 9.
73. *Gorgias*, 527d in Plato, *The Collected Dialogues*, edited by Edith Hamilton
    and Huntington Cairns, Bollingen Series, LXXI, Princeton University
    Press, Princeton, 1969, p. 307.

CHAPTER 2

A "Therapy of Self-Examination": [1]
The Psychological Method

For the words "holy fear" signify the act of will by which we shall inevitably refuse to sin and also guard against sin, not because of any anxiety about our weakness for fear that we may sin, but because of a calmness of mind that is the effect of love.

The City of God, XIV, 9

For in this region of weakness and in these evil days such anxiety is also not without its uses in causing them to seek with a keener longing that place of safety where peace is not complete and assured.

The City of God, XIX, 10

Through his *Confessions*, Augustine hoped to open to others some of the secrets that had been made known to him. An understanding of his own psyche had led him to an awareness of the psychological dimensions of the social, political, and religious problems of his day. He had then to confront these problems as a public figure in Hippo. The framework in which he operated was, of course, religious. His was a religion that was a part of the society and politics of fourth-century Roman North Africa. Thus his success as an edifying writer and as a preacher depended upon a subtle combination of theology and psychology.

Roman praxis had denied people a sense of unity and wholeness through which they might struggle against the enervating and dispiriting aspects of Roman culture. Much like Plato, Augustine thought that if reason dominated the passions, an inner light would illuminate that which was true, enabling the rational man to execute judgment and righteousness. The problem was that most individuals lacked the self-confidence, integrity, and dignity that had to accompany—if not pre-cede—such judgment. Roman citizens would, however, have first to understand that Roman culture sought to deny their independence and their happiness.

Augustine had found a representation of true unity within himself. He had needed time to realize the psychological wholeness which that unity promised, but during that time he came to understand its accessibility to all who would look. There are, he believed, three distinct aspects of the self that combine to form its essential unity.

> The three things of which I speak are, to Be, to Know, and to Will. For I am, I know, and I Will; I am Knowing, and Willing, and I know myself to Be and to Will: and I Will to Be and to Know. In these three, there-fore, let him who can see how inseparable a life there is—even one life, one mind and one essence; finally how inseparable is the distinction yet a distinction.[2]

In his youth, willing, knowing, and being seemed always to struggle with one another, leaving him uncertain and anxious. That which he was conflicted with what he willed and what he knew. Moreover his knowledge and his will were in conflict with one another.

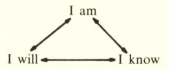

Indeed the struggle between knowing and willing raged on throughout most of his life.

Augustine sought to manage this struggle knowing full well that human beings were incomplete and unable to find psychological or social perfection in this life. But he emphasized that ethical action—knowing what is right and willfully acting upon the basis of that knowl-edge—is both possible and important in the face of life's incompleteness. Still, he knew that for many, commitment to action that promised only partial rewards in this world and nothing for the next would be diffi-cult. Many would be tempted by the arguments of those who promised more. Others would be easily frustrated by the burdens of self-exami-nation.

Underlying all of these problems was the inescapable anxiety of human existence. The success of his teaching thus depended upon its ability to confront that anxiety. It had to demonstrate that the claims of those who offer false hope are invalidated because of their failure to confront human imperfection and the anxiety that accompanies it. It needed, as well, to justify the pursuit of moral excellence in the face of human limitation, anxiety, and inevitable counsels of despair.

In the *Confessions,* Augustine walked a narrow path between hope and despair, worrying that an overdose of either could stifle human action. The discussion is very different in tone from that of *De Doctrina Christiana* where Augustine speaks directly of the use of "the fear of God [to] lead us to thought of our mortality and of our future death and so subdue human pride." [3] His *Confessions* are, as well, crafted so as to produce uncertainty and malaise verging on despair, but the discussion there is more indirect and subtle. Rather than speaking directly of fear, Augustine introduces examples of the tensions and torments of his own youth in order to illustrate the folly of human pride. In the process, he reveals both the glory of God's creation and the desperate condition of human beings who fail to recognize that glory. His aim is to awaken hope in his reader, even as he speaks despairingly of his own youthful corruption. Augustine's examination of his own life thus becomes an example. Careful self-examination of the sort that Augustine demonstrates in his *Confessions* will lead people to discover both the limits of human action and the great—though often unperceived—potential of the human will and of human action in this world.

He sought to this end to develop what one commentator has called a "therapy of self-examination"—a therapy that would allow others, as he had been allowed, to understand more fully the nature of the world in which they lived and acted. Or as he put it he sought

> a remedy for the soul, which is provided by divine providence and unspeakable kindness. . . . It is divided into authority and reason. Authority demands faith and prepares man for reason. Reason leads to understanding and knowledge. Although reason never utterly forsakes authority: . . . still since we have come to temporalities and are hindered from the eternal by love of them, *a certain temporal remedy which calls not those who know, but those who believe, to health has a priority not in the order of nature and perfection, but in the order of time* [4] (emphasis added).

This initial remedy, as Augustine developed it in his *Confessions,* would help strengthen the individual (being) so he could use reason to understand more fully both human and divine order. This new understanding (and knowing) would better allow man to act "willfully" in the world. But to achieve this new dignity and integrity, he had first to believe—to subordinate himself through faith, to establish the boundaries within which he could willfully act. Only then could "being" be restored to a unity with "willing" and "knowing."

His being was defined in relation to the absolute standards of God, and his willing and knowing were, as well, more clearly placed. More confident that knowledge could bring order and peace to his life, his will was more sharply directed in the service of that knowledge.

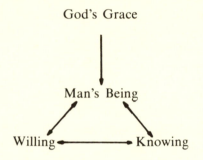

Being thus manages tension between willing and knowing, but only after being is defined and in turn has focused more clearly the purpose of knowing and willing.

Augustine's task in the *Confessions* was to reopen to the individual the possibility of this kind of being and to introduce its potential force even "in the midst of the earth." Our task in this chapter is to examine the character of Augustine's "therapy" and his use of anxiety as a part of that therapy. Anxiety was a necessary part of people's lives, and he offers them the means to face it. In the process, anxiety took on a creative potential in that it could—if properly perceived—challenge people and lead not to paralysis but to an active search for self-realization.[5]

It was not enough for Augustine simply to offer an alternative to Rome and Roman standards of moral judgment. The Platonists had such an alternative—one that he admired—but they had had little success, he felt, in changing people's understanding of themselves. They had a vision of the truth that impressed him, but they had no clear understanding of the way in which to attain that vision. As he noted in Book VII of the *Confessions:*

> It is one thing, from the mountain's wooded summit to see the land of peace, and not to find the way there—in vain to attempt impassable ways, opposed and waylaid by fugitives and deserters, under their captain the lion and the dragon; and another to keep to the way that leads there, guarded by the host of the heavenly general. . . .[6]

One of his chief tasks in the *Confessions* was to offer, through his example, such a way. Again it was a way that would provide both "a remedy for the Soul" and "a certain temporal remedy." He hoped that Christian charity would eventually provide a practicable alternative, but he was convinced that people would have first to be prepared very carefully. Only if people were first made to question the codes that governed their lives, could they be taught the necessity of adopting a new code. Here again the sophistication of Augustine's therapy must be fully recognized. He sought to develop a critical perspective for his readers and for his congregants, but he knew that that perspective must be elicited without creating cynicism and cynical withdrawal. Augustine's goal was to involve people in a search for new standards, even as the old were cast aside.

To this end Augustine began to develop what has been described as the creative potential in human anxiety.[7] Anxiety was the result of the fundamentally dependent nature of the human condition. But, he insisted, human dependence is complex and must be carefully understood. Human beings are dependent in at least two general ways. First, of course, they are dependent upon God as their creator and as the source of all order.[8] In addition, they are dependent as well upon various human institutions.[9] It is this second sort of dependence that Augustine sets out to investigate in the early books of his *Confessions*. Moreover, it is this sort of dependence that Augustine sees as the source of human anxiety.

Here again, the discussion is not as explicit as that in *De Doctrina Christiana*. Still, as Augustine searches his own past in the *Confessions*, he attempts to induce in his readers an understanding of their own dependence and to make them anxious about unnecessary dependence on corrupt human institutions. In *De Doctrina*, he speaks directly of the need to use human institutions, but warns that those institutions must be used carefully and guided by a higher authority.[10] Through the *Confessions*, the reader is indirectly led to examine those institutions— family and school, as well as the social and political order generally—in intensely personal terms. That examination is intended by Augustine to create anxiety that will impel him to seek a more ordered use of those institutions in the service of *caritas*.

Authority and Anxiety

Augustine's therapeutic process begins, therefore, with a careful examination of human dependence on other human beings and human institutions. That dependence is the result of original sin, and so is a necessary facet of the human condition. Human weakness—from the time of Adam forward—requires the nurturance, Augustine insisted, that comes with authoritative counsel and instruction. The problem is that such counsel and instruction varies widely, and is not always nurturant. It can in fact be destructive. An infant's relationship to his parents, a child's relationship to his teachers, a citizen's relationship to a ruler—[11] each of these describes a situation of human dependence introduced by Augustine in Book I of his *Confessions*. Each has the potential to provide nurturant counsel and instruction, but each relationship could deteriorate as well. As was the case with all human institutions, Augustine felt that these could be used well or poorly, depending upon the end toward which they were directed. Augustine sought to redirect human institutions from *cupiditas* to *caritas*.

Thus an important element of anxiety accompanied all relationships in which dependent people needed the guidance of wise authority. The problem for Augustine lay in the character of that wise authority. What is wisdom? Who is wise? In the absence of true standards, the choice among competing authorities would be an unnecessarily anxious one. Augustine's reflections about the confusing—often conflicting—advice from his parents, teachers, and friends illustrate the dilemma. He knew that one could never be totally certain of the rightness of human counsel, but he thought that one could at least minimize the debilitating aspects of the anxiety that uncertainty produced.

Indeed, Augustine understood very clearly the fundamental ambivalence that is a part of every relation of authority. Even a tiny infant rebelled against the authority of its parents, however clear the need for protection and nurturance may have been to all involved in the relationship.[12] The problem would not diminish as he passed from infancy to childhood and on into the "troublesome society of human businesses." [13] Dependence on the authority of his parents and his elders, however necessary, became no less difficult to accept. The rightness of their counsel was no more certain.

Augustine's own parents had failed in their advice to their son to confront the most basic questions of his disgruntled youth, for they did not understand the broader social, political, and moral roots of his disorder.[14] Rather, their concern for his private success as a student and teacher served only to reinforce anomic feelings engendered by a corrupt Roman culture. In order to be truly effective, Augustine reasoned, parental advice must develop as the result of carefully articulated and commonly accepted standards of judgment about a good social order. Such advice could minimize the destructive aspects of anxiety, for it gave the individual the sense that he was a part of a common endeavor, and could have the support of others in the same situation.

Even the best authoritative relationship would produce a certain amount of anxiety, but if the conditions were right, that anxiety might not produce personal confusion. Moreover, if the counsel provided by an authority is properly structured, it might open to the person being counselled the possibility of a new ordering of his life and the lives of those around him. Augustine's great teacher, St. Ambrose, had provided him with such guidance. Gentle and yet firm, Ambrose taught Augustine that he had broken with the larger order of nature, and would have to recognize the True Authority that presided over that order. Only the acknowledgment of that authority would permit an individual to overcome the prideful temptations of a corrupt Roman culture.[15]

Ambrose was for Augustine an authority who compelled his pupil to recognize his limitations and to strive positively within those limits. Augustine sought to emulate his teacher, instructing his students that although dependence was inevitable, it would—if properly understood—help them to recognize that they bore unnecessarily many of the burdens of Roman society. They would have to learn first, however, that others shared their burdens. They could then seek in a communal setting positive standards of duty and goodness. This recognition would open them to a more secure sense of personal and social identity and make their need for authority more understandable.

Augustine worried that the standards of public virtue that guided the world of late antiquity produced "corrosive anxieties" [16] that blinded people to even the possibility of human excellence. Dominated by these anxieties, individuals would be incapable of pursuing truth. Lacking true standards of judgment, they would be doomed to uncertainty and superficiality. Concerned about securing their possessions, motivated by cries of "well done, well done," [17] they viewed the world in private and selfish terms. This perspective radically limited their vision of the common good. Furthermore, it gave them little hope of assistance in their anxious efforts to sustain their publicly acclaimed positions. Anxiety about social and economic status limits one's vision, estranging a person from his fellows and stunting the development of the self. Here the self is defined by external objects and opinions over which it has little control. Rather than seeking wholeness, this anxiety-ridden individual revels in his incompleteness and is rendered incapable of aid.

By contrast, the anxiety that Augustine defended engages the individual in the therapeutic process of the *Confessions*.[18] Much later in the *City of God* he would argue that "anxiety is not without its uses in causing [people] to seek with a keener eye that place of safety where peace is most complete and assured." [19] In the *Confessions,* he established the psychological foundations for such later observations. The recognition of human dependence on God produces anxiety, but it is accompanied by standards of judgment—e.g., the scriptures and the example of Christ—that allow the individual to search for new ways of coping with human weakness. He will thus better understand the uses and limits of reason. He will be humbled by that which is beyond human comprehension, yet energized by the recognition that reason can be used in the service of *caritas* instead of *cupiditas.*

There is, therefore, for Augustine, a qualitative difference between those "corrosive anxieties" that dominated Roman culture and that true anxiety that resulted from a recognition of absolute dependence on God. A recognition of this second sort of anxiety would literally ease the burdens of the first. The creative potential of the second anxiety lay in its ability to force an individual to confront the psychological tyranny of Rome, so that he might be freed to discover a sense of measure and proportion within himself.[20] Then, more certain about his own identity and his own judgments, he might begin to liberate himself from the superficial and privatizing standards of Roman society.

It was Augustine's aim to influence people to act, not just to think and pray, but to serve *caritas* and the good of all. He had come to understand that the false self-confidence that grew in the pursuit of wealth and empire had blinded and deafened many around him. He hoped to teach people a new and more disciplined way of coping with their existence. But in order to be successful, he had to provide leadership of a sort very different from that commonly exercised in Roman North Africa on all levels of society. He offered, that is, a new model of authority.

Driven to anxious self-examination both before and after his conversion, Augustine offered—through his example and through his teaching—a new hope to many who had been unwittingly entrapped by the powerful if superficial lure of Rome and Roman custom. Seeking "honor among men and deceitful riches," Augustine and his young friends remained unaware of the limitations of human freedom.[21] Ironically, this failure to recognize the limits of human freedom resulted in a distorted vision of it—a vision that in the end rendered them all less free. Unselfconscious and unaware, they became prisoners of a "chain of habit"—a chain that was the creation of their own misguided wills. Freedom to act apart from that habit would come only after their wills were redirected. Augustine hoped to provide that direction for others in the way Ambrose had for him.

Augustine, of course, assumed a great burden here, for it was his duty to help lead people through this program of self-criticism and self-examination. He was aware that this was no easy task, but he warned of the dangers of being silent even in the face of difficulty. It was not enough simply to make people self-consciously critical of existing standards and institutions. The very process of criticism must lead them to seek alternatives. The therapeutic process in the *Confessions* was designed by Augustine to accomplish precisely this. We must now turn to the early books of the *Confessions* for a closer look at the beginnings of his therapy and the nature of the anxiety that he elicited.

Augustine's Example—The Tears of Infants and the Games of Children

According to Augustine, an infant develops an urge to control those around him after being confronted with his own weakness.[22] Recalling his own childhood, Augustine wrote in Book I of his *Confessions* that when his desires asserted themselves,

> I would cast about limbs and voice, making the few and feeble signs I could, like, though indeed not much what I wished; and when I was not satisfied—either not understood, or because it would have been injurious to me—grew I indignant that my elders were not subject to me, and that those on whom I had no claim did not wait on me, and avenged myself on them by tears.[23]

Thus is established the basic dependency of the human species and the beginning of the search to overcome it. Early attempts are gross. Unsophisticated and insensitive, the infant Augustine described knew only that the world around him challenged him. His position was, however, naturally weak, and his choice of weapons limited. The lack of development was crucial to Augustine's account, for it suggested a place to begin the most basic task of education—the education of the will, a will over which even the infant had some control. It further suggested a natural setting within which that education might begin— that of the natural dependence within the family.

Education, Augustine stressed, is crucial to the situation. It could, however, develop in two very different directions. It could be an education that helped the child to understand the nature of his dependencies and weaknesses, or it could be a miseducation that might crush him.

Augustine looked to the authority of parents and elders as fundamental for the most basic foundation of education. He examined, for example, the workings of his childhood memory, as it helped him to learn how to speak and to think.

> So it was that by frequently hearing words, in duly placed sentences, I gradually gathered what things they were signs of; and having formed

my mouth to the utterance of these signs, I thereby expressed my will. Thus I exchanged with those about me the signs by which we express our wishes and advanced deeper into the *stormy fellowship of human life, depending all the while on the authority of parents, and the beck of elders.*[24] (emphasis added).

Education—facilitated by a child's rational capacities and in particular his use of words—could now begin to shape his sense of self more directly. But, the "stormy fellowship of human life," we are told, demands obedience to those in authority. At the very instant, then, that the child gains self-consciousness and asserts his independence, the profundity of his dependence is demonstrated to him. If he is to command the attention of others and control the situation in which he finds himself, the child will be increasingly dependent upon language and thus dependent on those who seem to master words and the rules that govern their use.

Rebellion would seem to be inevitable, for the more fully rational capacities develop, the more powerful will be the temptation to use them to establish power over the wills of others. The contradiction is clear, Augustine warns, because others will be comparably tempted. The need for human institutions that maintain order becomes obvious. This formal need, however, is only the first step. Augustine wants his reader to recognize from the start that the real issue at stake here is the quality of those institutions—the nature of the order that they provide and the education they offer in the service of that order.

Augustine was highly critical of the human institutions that lent order to his early life and of the lessons about freedom and authority they taught. He notes that students feared their teachers, but seldom respected them. Teachers in turn were inconsistent—even hypocritical. Punishing students for truancy and for play, they themselves lived their lives as players of games. "But," he continues, "elder folks idlenesses must, forsooth, be called business, and when children do the like, the same men must punish them. . . ."[25]

Hypocrisy was, however, only the beginning. Augustine also criticized the substantive content of his lessons. Speaking of lascivious fables that he and his fellows were forced to memorize, he points to the "wine of error" delivered to them by his "intoxicated teachers." This teaching not only failed to provide the moral instruction that would allow students to cope with the "stormy fellowship of human society," but it actually threatened the very foundation of that society. His teacher took "no heed at all" of the destructive moral and social consequences of this false instruction, but rather worried only "that his tongue trips not before men."[26] Augustine had become dependent upon men whom he could not respect. He had been taught in turn that respect was won only through a "copious and neat oration." [27] Anxious to avoid the rod, he slavishly followed the rules and customs of the day.

The young Augustine learned his lessons well, and was recognized as among the best in the techniques of rhetoric. Yet he regularly disobeyed "out of a desire to play: aspiring to be captain in all sports, and to have mine ears tickled with feigned fables, to make them itch the more glowingly: the like desperate curiosity also sparking through mine eyes, after the shows and plays of my elders. . . ." [28] The lessons that those elders taught were only superficially linked to the development of an independent and tempered will. Rebellion and disorder were inevitable. Indeed, Augustine and his compatriots deceived "tutors and masters and parents" with innumerable lies. Their deceptions suggested more than the love of play—they were imitating the stage plays of their elders.[29]

Human authority is the necessary result of original sin, but it is not inevitable that that authority be worthy of respect. In his *Confessions,* Augustine attempts to teach his reader of the necessity of such authority and of the need to judge the righteousness of the instruction that any given authority offers. To this end he explores the possibilities and liabilities that inhere in family and friendship. From the games of children he turns to the awesome tasks of parental guidance and the burdensome responsibilities of fraternal loyalty.

Augustine's Example—The Carnal Affection of Parents and Friends

Augustine's discussion of parental authority lies at the heart of his *Confessions.* From general comments about the responsibilities of parents in Book I, Augustine passes to specific references to both his father and mother in the following eight books. In fact, Augustine's relationship with his parents—especially to this mother, Monnica—provides dramatic continuity to the entire autobiographical section of his *Confessions.* His dependence upon his parents, rebellion against them, and love for them are intermixed throughout, thus providing a clear focus from which to measure changes in Augustine's life. Moreover, his portrayal of these relationships affords him the opportunity to introduce in concrete terms the nature of his youthful anxiety.

Like his teachers, his parents' main concern was that he "learn to make a powerful oration, and to prove a most persuasive speaker." [30] Their ambition for his success blinded them to the responsibilities of authoritative guidance. Even the turbulent pressures and passions of his adolescence were addressed by his parents in terms of their son's budding rhetorical career. His father's responsibility is minimal, we are told, because he "was but a catechumen, one newly converted." [31] Thus he did not—in Augustine's eyes—understand his responsibility to direct his son beyond the worldly success that the passing fashion of fourth-century Roman North Africa applauded.

Monnica on the other hand had grander ambitions for Augustine that transcended mere worldly success. Still, she too was unable to provide good counsel because she was likewise guided by hopes *"not . . . of the next world . . .* but the hopes of learning, [things of this world] which both [his] parents were greatly desirous I should attain to" (emphasis added). Lacking consistent advice from his parents, he reports that he relied on the impudence of friends to guide him through the difficult years of adolescence.

> I ran headlong with such blindness, that I was ashamed among my equals to be guilty of less impudency than they were, whom I heard brag mightily of their naughtiness: yea, and so much the more boasting, by how much more they had been beastly: and I took pleasure to do it, not for the pleasure of the act only, but for the praise of it also.[32]

Monnica eventually lost touch with her son and would not realize her true ambitions for him for nine long years.[33] It is most apparent that Augustine sees his mother as a significant hindrance to his growth. He would deceive her and escape the bonds of her "carnal affection" [34] toward him by sneaking off to Rome. However fondly she doted on his company, she was unable to advise her son. Her advice in fact "seemed to me no better than women's advices, which would be a shame for me to follow." [35] He had begun this very discussion of his mother with a plea for order in his life. Her carnal affection for him had rendered her incapable of providing instruction in the principles of that order.[36] To a great extent, it seemed responsible for his inner turmoil and his desire to separate from her. Though she appears to have offered more direction to his life than his father or any other male authority figure, she could not by herself deal with her son's complex needs and demands. Only after Ambrose began to offer Augustine the counsel and instruction he had lacked, would Augustine and his mother—individually and together—understand the difficulties of their early years.

"Oh for someone to have regulated my disorder," he exhorts, "and turned to my profit the fleeting beauties of the things around me." [37] Those around him took no care to sort out their ambitions for him from his own most pressing emotional needs. His parents responded to his discontent by slackening the reins of liberty "beyond all temper of severity, yea even to dissoluteness which brought the various troubles." [38] Augustine was unprepared for this liberality and became more dependent upon the opinion of his fellows. He became more anxious, lest he not fulfill their expectations. But this was a destructive anxiety that inhibited the very process of discovery and growth.

Left to his own devices, Augustine sought affection in other places. The result was anxiety, confusion, unhappiness, even despair.

> I was delighted in nothing, he says, save to love and be loved. But I held it not in moderation, mind to mind, the bright path of friendship, but out of the dark concupiscence of flesh and the effervescence of youthful exhaltations came forth which obscured and overcast my heart, so that I was unable to discern pure affection from unholy desire.[39]

His need to be loved was consuming and clearly misdirected. Once again his very being was distorted by a will unable to withstand the temptation of superficial passion.

He was apparently unable to move beyond that notion of friendship-as-peer-approval that had in his sixteenth year led him to commit the senseless theft of a pear.[40] He had been enticed by inferior beauties and led by his desire to win the affection of his fellows. "Alone," he reports, "I would never have done it. Belike therefore it was the company that I loved, who were with me at it." [41] None of these were true friends, nor were they truly loved, for they were all used to gratify selfish desires or to justify greed. He describes this sort of friendship in Book II:

> O friendship too unfriendly! Thou inscrutable inveigler of the soul, thou greediness to do mischief, all out of a mirth and wantonness, thou thirst to do wrong to others, though upon no pleasure of gain or revenge unto me: but even because when one cries: Let us go, let us do this or that, then 'tis a shame not to be shameless.[42]

His desire to love and be loved would grow in the early years of his adult life, but not beyond the bounds of selfishness that had been established at this early time. He loved an orator, he says, "because of the love of those who praised him." [43] Trapped all the while by the passing judgment of the crowd for whom the orator performed, Augustine envied rather the praise of the crowd than the substance of the oration. He was still prone to falling in love with inferior beauties.[44]

Even more disquieting, though, was his grief at the deathbed of one to whom he had come to feel very close. The death of his friend and the loss of fraternal support produced anguish for Augustine. He wept

bitterly—unhappy in life and yet fearful of death. "I still thought,"
he reports, "my soul and his soul to have been but one soul in two
bodies. . . . And even there perchance was I afraid to die, lest he should
wholly die, whom so passionately I had loved." [45] What then was the
source of his bitterness? He laments losing a half of himself, and is
angry and hurt less at the loss of a friend than at a part of himself. "Is
weeping a bitter thing," he asks, because it reflects "my lost joy?" [46]
Anger at losing what was before enjoyed might be the true source of
grief. Augustine had valued his friend not as a distinct person, but for
the joy he provided and as a prop to bolster an insecure sense of
himself.

Augustine would learn that friendship of this sort, far from providing
that mutual support in which "each pilgrim bearing along the way the
other's burden," made such mutual support almost impossible. The
anxieties attendant to transitory human existence and the partial loves
that it too often inspires were indeed very powerful.

> Let not my soul be fastened unto these things with the glue of love
> through the senses of my body. For these things go whither they were to
> go, that they might no longer be; and they cleave the soul in sunder with
> most pestilent desires: even because the soul earnestly desires to be one
> with them, and loves finally to rest in these things which she loves. But in
> those things she finds not settlement, which are still fleeing, because they
> stand not: they flee away; and who is he that can follow them with the
> senses of his flesh; yea, who is able to overtake them, when they are hard
> by him? [47]

His only hope was to look for a friendship not so dependent upon
selfish needs, but where was he to look? Roman culture offered instruction only in vicarious affection, in the false friendship of thieves, or the
friendship of those superficially linked in a crowd.

The Catharsis of Public Spectacle

Public expressions of emotion were a regular part of Roman life, but
they offered little to one who sought true friendship. Thus stage plays
were a favorite target of Augustine. They did nothing but fire his fan-
tasy life and further intensify those affections that had enslaved him.
The emotions elicited during these plays were, he thought, totally con-
trived. Feelings of pity or mercy, for example, were felt only at a distance and never acted upon.

> But what kind of mercy is it that arises from fictitious and scenic pas-
> sions? The hearer is not expected to relieve, but merely invited to grieve;

and the more he grieves, the more he applauds the actor of these fictions. And if the misfortunes of the characters whether of olden times or merely imaginary, be so represented as not to touch the feelings of the spectator, he goes away disgusted and censorious; but if his feelings be touched, he sits out attentively, and sheds tears of joy.[48]

It was precisely this combination of play acting and "spectating"—endowed with a kind of legitimacy by the stage play—that Augustine had found so reprehensible in his childhood. Much like Rousseau would later argue in his letter to D'Alembert,[49] Augustine felt that both the passivity of the spectator and the contrivances of the actor were potentially damaging to civic virtue.

Emotions were totally recast in this setting. Misery had become someone else's grief—a grief to be applauded if it was severe enough, a grief perhaps that made one forget one's own. Mercy had become empty compassion, pity, perhaps contempt. It was surely not the source of affectionate concern, because it was something over which one was led to shed tears of joy.

Augustine, by contrast, offers a different lesson in public behavior. He himself becomes a respected public authority, holding up before his audience an example that they will easily understand in its weakness, and will admire in its resolve to confront the most debilitating aspects of that weakness. His writing and his preaching were thus a new kind of public spectacle. He taught people that there were things that could be achieved on this earth, and he urged all ministers to teach that lesson. Near the end of the *Confessions* he prays.

> Now therefore let thy ministers work upon this Earth . . . and let them be a pattern unto the faithful, by living before them, and by *stirring them up to imitation. For thus do men hear, not so as to hear only, but to do also* [50] (emphasis added).

These public teachings might stir emotions as effectively as the Roman theater, but never for applause. They sought not to entertain spectators, but to engage an audience in common action toward the good of all. This end was alien to the stage player and even more removed from other public spectacles.

Similarly, Augustine knew directly of the demonic character of Roman spectacles. He looks back with horror, for example, at the attraction that frivolous public displays held for his friend Alypius, and he reports that these spectacles induced an atmosphere of violence and madness that seemed to transform his friend Alypius.

> He looked on, he cried out for company, he was inflamed with it, carried home such a measure of madness as spurred him on to come another time: and that not only in their company who first haled him on, but to run before them too, yea, and hale on others also.[51]

The crowd he was with and the spectacle that inflamed him had literally overcome his being. Once again it is clear that Augustine finds in Roman spectacles generally a metaphor of the larger society that he is attacking—a society that has as well overcome the very being of its citizens.

Augustine's unique method of instruction through public confession challenged both the form and the substance of these Roman plays and games. Offering instruction in neither public nor private virtue, they provided only catharsis. Augustine sought not simply to replace them, but to attack those aspects of Roman character—both individual and collective—that justified them and made them necessary. He knew that alternatives to Roman culture that offered only new forms of spectacle or eloquence were suspect.

Augustine had been tempted thus by the promises of the Manicheans. His flirtation with them is described by him as an attempt to find definite answers—to justify his own life through some kind of external intervention that would free him from responsibility.

> For it still seemed to me that it was not we that sin, but that I knew not what other nature sinned in us. And it gratified my pride to be free from blame, and, after I had committed any fault, not to acknowledge that against Thee; but I loved to excuse it, and accuse something else (I know not what) which was with me, but I was not.[52]

Such a view could neither diagnose nor treat either Rome's maladies or Augustine's. On the contrary, it fed that very pride that was at the heart of both disorders.

Still, he was tempted by them. Having found the scriptures unworthy and having looked upon himself as a "great one," he "fell among men proudly raving, very carnal and voluble in whose mouth were the snares of the devil. . . ." Theirs was a convincing message. He longed to have the problems of his identity resolved—his place in an immense and complicated Roman world firmly established. Faustus—the great Manichean leader for whom Augustine had long waited—would, he hoped, offer such self-justification.

> When at last he did come, I found him to be a man of pleasant speech, who spoke of the very same things they [other members of the sect] did, although more fluently, and in better language. But of what profit to me

was the elegance of my cup-bearer, since he offered me not the more precious draught for which I thirsted? [53]

In fact, Faustus offered Augustine little more than Roman public festivals. Once again he had been disappointed by the offerings of friends and companions. Self-justification and identity would not be easily found. The negative experience of his young adulthood seemed increasingly inadequate.

Augustine's Example—From Negative to Positive Anxiety

Augustine's family had offered him neither the authority nor the affection that he so desperately needed. Early efforts at friendship proved equally wanting as guides to self-respect and genuinely reciprocal love. Roman culture provided occasional releases for pent-up emotional energy, but they offered little support for those like Augustine who had begun to seek a happiness beyond the superficial rewards of public acclaim and material gain. Finally, the Manichees failed to confront his most pressing anxieties. Still—in each of these and earlier experiences—he had learned something that he could convey to his reader.

Augustine believed that human beings grow only through a testing that is often painful and—quite literally—disillusioning. Even the common error of childhood was turned, he notes, to "learning, to [his] own benefit; and [his] error" used for his "punishment." [54] Monnica waited many years during which her "patience and meekness" [55] were sorely tested by a "scourge of sorrows." [56] Augustine too would suffer during this time as he "tumbled up and down over the mind of that deep pit, and the darkness of [the] false belief" that was Manicheanism. Deluded time and again by false liberty, false friendship, and dishonest students, he sought reassurance only to be "violently . . . flung down again." [57] Yet neither gives up! "Yea," he insists, "the very pleasures of our human life do we procure by preceding difficulties." "The greatest joy is everywhere ushered in by the greatest painfulness." [58]

Augustine is, of course, well aware of the dangers inherent in this human experience. Hard times might provoke personal growth, but only if those hard times are understood and prepared for very carefully. People must not be allowed to wallow in a self-pity that blocks the path to self-understanding and Christian charity. Divine providence may be ultimately responsible for both the difficulties and the joys of human existence, but it is likewise clear that people are carefully prepared through the intervention of other human beings. Monnica learns very slowly—and with the assistance of Bishop Ambrose—of her early errors in judgment. She perseveres, but with growing understanding of "her own country custom" and of the dangers of the carnal senses.[59] Augustine also requires the assistance of friends and associates, and especially the guidance of Ambrose, to wean him away from the "brightest beam of material light"[60] and the shallowness of the "market place of loquacity."[61] Alypius is taught by his experiences in Rome, but these were, Augustine reports, "laid up in his memory for a medicine" later on.[62] It would take the intervention of an old acquaintance and eventually that of Augustine himself to act as catalytic agents. Only then would Alypius become "knit in with [Augustine] with a most strong tie" so they might jointly and without jealousy seek after truth and wisdom.[63]

For Augustine—the therapist—the memory is a valuable storehouse of experience from which the individual may learn and develop. The problem for Augustine was to secure the release of that information. He suggests that times of crisis—Monnica's "scourge of sorrow" or his own outrage at the cynicism of his students in Carthage and Rome—could help by shocking people into self-consciousness. This self-consciousness will truly help, however, only if someone is there to guide that understanding beyond the specific crises at hand. Again, the quality of authoritative counsel and instruction is crucial.

Augustine argues throughout his *Confessions* that Roman culture of the late fourth century was designed to promote insecurity without any remedy. Rome's very existence depended upon standards of public judgment that were constantly shifting and uncertain. Whether one sought status through the accumulation of material goods or through the acclaim granted by opinion, one always had to be cautious and uncertain. Having defined his very being in terms of objects and fashions that were only indirectly subject to his control, he had constantly to look outside of himself for an understanding of who he was. The process of self-examination in which Augustine engaged and that he sought to teach his reader could not even begin under such circumstances. Under the sway of Roman standards of excellence, Augustine's North African could never learn the source of the fundamental confusion, insecurity, and anxiety that Augustine himself had felt.

Insofar as the Manicheans failed to confront these same questions, they too were found wanting. "I began to despair," says Augustine, "that [the great Manichean teacher—Faustus] should ever open and untie these difficulties which so perplexed me."[64] Likewise, the skepticism of the Ciceronian Academy—though it gave him a weapon with which to attack the Manichees—[65] failed to address his most pressing problems—his disappointments as a teacher of rhetoric and his uncertainty about the most basic direction of his life.

The successful unmasking of Roman institutions and Manichean doctrine demanded another sort of anxiety that would compel rather than inhibit a search for psychological and political wholeness. Augustine, his mother, his friends, and his readers would have to look now for new standards through which to judge human excellence. The search would prove difficult indeed! Augustine tells us, for example, of his efforts with Alypius with whom "he sighed" and "wavered," searching for happiness and asking the most difficult of questions.[66] Or again of the time, when joined by other friends, he plotted to continue his search in an isolated intellectual community.

> And we were many friends, which debated together, conferring about the detesting these turbulent molestations of human life; and we had now almost resolved to sequester ourselves from company, and to live at peace: we hoped to obtain that peace by putting together what stock every man was able to make, and making one household of all: that through the plain dealing of common friendship, one thing should not be this man's and another thing that man's; but what stock should be made up out of every man's particular, should in the whole belong unto the interest of every single person, and all together, unto all in general.[67]

An admirable plan, Augustine suggests, but one that we ourselves destroyed, no sooner had we begun to discuss whether or not our wives would join us. Divided again, they returned to their "old sighings and groanings and wanderings." The true way to wisdom had not yet been discovered. Augustine and his companions were again filled with restlessness and anxiety in their quest for peace, but they had now at least begun the quest in earnest.

In Milan under the guidance of Bishop Ambrose, the search continued as Augustine became a catechumen, but his growing knowledge of Christianity was still couched in the philosophical terms of Neoplatonism.[68] Such understanding as he gained, he suggests, caused him to become "more and more puffed up with . . . knowledge," confusing "presumption and confession," that is the presumption of "those that saw whither they were to go, but knew nothing of the way," and the confession of praise that offers "that *path* which leads unto that blessed country, not only to be looked upon, but dwelt in." [69] As yet, his philosophic musings had produced few concrete results. An alternative—such as the Platonists imagined and described—had little significance for Augustine, unless it produced more than mere contemplation. However important Augustine found contemplation, he learned early that it had to be supplemented by explicit action. That is, the new standards of judgment that it offered had to produce action based on those standards.

Augustine came to this understanding in Milan when, he reports, he was set face to face with himself finally. Having heard the story of one Ponticianus who told of his conversion to Christianity and compared his postconversion service to Christ with his previous service to the Roman State and emperor, Augustine is introduced to a new certainty. Taken "from behind my back, where I had heretofore placed myself, whenas I had no list to observe mine own self," he was finally set face to face with himself, he proclaims, and was forced to "reflect upon myself." [70] Still held prisoner by the sway of custom, he dramatically reveals the beginnings of a new and profound self-understanding. His long struggle was nearing its end. Soon, the many and confused pieces of his twelve-year search would begin to fit together. The errors of his early life would be placed in a new perspective, and a new life—apart from carnal affection and material delight—would be opened up before him. He would, to be sure, never experience complete liberation from those delights and affections, but he could now at the least understand something of the slavish hold over his life that they held. Thus Augustine can offer to his reader the possibility that the "odyssey of the soul" [71] through self-examination can conclude in relief and hope.

Temptation, of course, remained for him and for his reader. Human beings would not through the process of self-examination lose their dependence on other human beings and human institutions. They could, however, learn a great deal about themselves and their institutions. Augustine argued that they have the potential to develop well beyond the generally accepted standards of public and private excellence of Roman North Africa in the late fourth century.

Freed from the enervating anxieties of Roman custom, Augustine and his reader are propelled by a new and creative anxiety to seek new principles of order and justice. The knowledge and understanding of those principles would come only very slowly, but the rewards would be great. Even as Augustine discovered his finitude and the limitation that his condition implied, he had begun to develop within those finite limits. Personal growth became more probable, as the boundaries of human action were more clearly defined. In order to understand those bounds more clearly, it is necessary now to turn to Augustine's conception of unity and order—the end toward which he attempts to move his reader in the final books of the *Confessions*.

Notes

1. Peter Brown, *Augustine of Hippo,* University of California Press, Berkeley, 1969, chapter 16. (Hippo). This essay is in no way an attempt to psychoanalyze Augustine. A series of articles in the *Journal for the Scientific Study of Religion,* University of Connecticut Press, Storrs, vol. V, nos. 1 and 2, fall 1965 and spring 1966, illustrates both the strengths and the weaknesses of such attempts. Burrell, in "Reading the Confessions," cited above, suggests rightly that psychological explanations have in many cases "pretentions to completeness" that must be carefully watched. They can be guilty as well of errors not unlike those described in the introduction, failing to recognize that Augustine "forged his ideas in the heat of disputations with infidels and schismatics and heretics" and that he "tested them . . . in concrete situations that arose from his multifarious concerns as a pastor at a time in history when civil power was tottering." (G.L. Caldwell, "Augustine's Critique of Human Justice," *A Journal of Church and State,* vol. II, no. 1, May 1960, pp. 7–25.) Much of his harshness must be seen in this context—a context that makes psychological analysis of his life and works more complicated than it may seem to be at first. Again our intention is not to psychoanalyze Augustine, but rather to insist with Philip Woollcett *(Journal for the Scientific Study of Religion,* vol. 5, p. 273) that "Augustine was the greatest psychologist of his time and probably for many centuries to come." His psychological sensitivity and sophistication form the basis for much of his analysis of politics and society and must be carefully examined, if that analysis is to be understood by the contemporary reader.
2. *St. Augustine's Confessions,* 2 vols., The Loeb Classical Library, 1912, XIII, 11. *(Confs.)*
3. *De Doctrina Christiana,* II, 7, J.P. Migne, vol. 34, p. 30. *(DDC)*
4. Cited by Frederick E. Van Fleteron, "Authority and Reason, Faith and Understanding in the Thought of St. Augustine," *Augustinian Studies,* vol. 4, 1973, pp. 61–62.
5. Ibid. See also Maurice Stein, Arthur Vidich, and David White, *Identity and Anxiety,* Free Press, Glencoe, Ill., p. 134. Neo-Freudian psychology has developed this notion of self-realization. Though its methods are different, the end that it seeks—the development of "a person's use of his talents, skills and powers to his satisfaction within the realm of his own freely expressed realistic set of values"—is very close to that which Augustine sought.
6. *Confs.,* VII, 21.
7. Rollo May describes one particularly Augustinian approach in the following reference to Niebuhr.

> Niebuhr makes anxiety the central concept of his theological doctrine of man. To Niebuhr every act of man, creative or destructive, involves some element of anxiety. Anxiety has its source in the fact that man is on one hand finite, involved like the animals in the contingencies and necessities of nature; but on the other hand has freedom. Unlike "the animals he sees his situation (of contingency) and anticipates its perils," and to this extent man transcends his finiteness (Stein, Vidch, and White, p. 162).

There is much here that is as well a summary of Augustine, yet the Bishop of Hippo was—in his public role—much more than a theologian. He moved well beyond a descriptive analysis of man's existential plight to plot a strategy through which men could be taught to overcome the most debilitating aspects of their anxiety. He too avoided a utopian formulation of a world without anxiety, but this did not prevent him from developing a positive function for anxiety that challenged men to a new ethical activism. It is useful as well in this context to examine contemporary efforts to deal with the same problem—this time within a more strictly psychological framework. Carl A. Whitaker and Thomas P. Malone, for example, discuss the nature of "positive anxiety" in the following.

> In contrast to negative anxiety, which arises out of psychopathology, positive anxiety occurs in an individual who finds himself in an interpersonal relationship within the matrix of which he perceives the possibility of better organizing his affect [growing]. In these instances, new and unorganized affect becomes mobilized for growth. Thus, the mobilization of potential for growth also takes the form of anxiety in therapeutic relationships. Because anxiety produces growth in these instances it is termed positive anxiety.

Augustine's therapeutic process was described in very different language but its fundamental position was similar. He sought to make just such creative use of anxiety while overcoming its more negative aspects.

8. This is, of course, the constant theme of the *Confessions*. See, for example, I, 4; IX, 10; or XIII, 23.
9. See, for example, *Confs.*, I, 8, or *DDC*, II, 20–27.
10. *DDC*, II, 20–27.
11. *Confs.*, I, 19.
12. Ibid., I, 7.
13. Ibid., I, 8.
14. See, for example, *Confs.*, I, 7, 9; II, 23; V, 8.
15. See, for example *Confs.*, V, 14, and Book VI.
16. *DDC*, IV, 3.
17. See *Confs.*, I, 13; X, 36.
18. See note 6 above.
19. *DDC*, XIX, 10.
20. Ibid., I, 14. See also II, 6; III, 8; IV, 4; IX, 3 and XIII, 2 for discussions of feigned, immoderate, or false liberty—as opposed to Christian liberty.
21. *Confs.*, I, 9.
22. Ibid., I, 7.
23. Ibid.
24. Ibid., I, 9.
25. Ibid.
26. Ibid., I, 18.
27. Ibid.
28. Ibid., I, 10.
29. Ibid.
30. Ibid., II, 2.
31. Ibid., II, 3.

32. Ibid.
33. Ibid., III, 2.
34. Ibid., V, 8.
35. Ibid., II, 2.
36. Ibid., V, 8. Though Augustine speaks of his having deceived Monnica when he left for Rome, there is no question but that she has, in his eyes, forced him to the deception. She too "doted on my company," he suggests. Like other mothers, her carnal pride in her son blinded her to the spiritual ambitions she had for him. It was not until she was on her death bed that either would overcome those carnal senses that dominated their relationship *(Confs.,* IX, 10).
37. Ibid., II, 2.
38. Ibid., II, 3.
39. Ibid., IV, 14. J. F. Monagle has argued that Augustine's search for friendship was a search for reciprocity. Early relationships were not truly reciprocal, he suggests. Eventually Augustine would come to realize the need for the social life that grew out of the mutuality of friendship. However, he knew little of the need for mutual support of one pilgrim for another in these early days. See J. F. Monagle, "Friendship in St. Augustine's Biography," *Augustinian Studies,* vol II, 1971, pp. 81ff.
40. Ibid., II, 4.
41. Ibid., II, 8.
42. Ibid., II, 9.
43. Ibid., IV, 14.
44. Ibid., IV, 13.
45. Ibid., IV, 6.
46. Ibid., IV, 5.
47. Ibid., V, 8. See also Monagle.
48. Ibid., III, 2.
49. Jean-Jacques Rousseau, *Politics and the Arts, Letter to M. D'Alembert on the Theater,* translated by Allan Bloom, Free Press, Glencoe, Ill., 1960; see, for example, Part VI, p. 57ff.
50. *Confs.,* XIII, 21.
51. *Confs.,* VI, 8.
52. *Confs.,* V, 14.
53. *Confs.,* V, 6.
54. *Confs.,* I, 12.
55. *Confs.,* IX, 9.
56. *Confs.,* V, 8.
57. *Confs.,* III, 2.
58. *Confs.,* VIII, 3.
59. *Confs.,* VI, 2.
60. Ibid., IX, 10.
61. Ibid., IX, 2.
62. Ibid., V, 7.
63. Ibid., VI, 10.
64. Ibid., V, 7.
65. Ibid., V, 10.
66. Ibid., VI, 10.

67. Ibid., VI, 14.
68. Ibid., VII, 17.
69. Ibid., VII, 20.
70. Ibid., VIII, 7.
71. See Robert J. O'Connell, *Saint Augustine's Confessions: The Odyssey of the Soul,* Harvard University Press, Cambridge, 1969.

CHAPTER 3

Unity, Order, and Love:
The Philosophical Method

For a body which consists of members, all of which are beautiful, is by far more beautiful than the several members individually are, by whose well-ordered union the whole is completed, though these members also be severally beautiful.

Confessions, XII, 20

Augustine's conversion introduced him to the possibility of the unity and order in himself and in the world. He gained thereby a new understanding of himself. He was at once part of that unity and order, and at the same time profoundly and painfully alienated from it. The perfection of God's order was a standard against which individuals and societies could measure themselves, even though it was a perfection that neither individuals nor societies could hope to attain in this life.

In the course of his *Confessions*, Augustine had in effect passed from anxiety to alienation. First anxious about the superficial opinions of elders and teachers and the fickle whims of students and friends, the young Augustine was unable to find even a modicum of happiness. Then—propelled by a new anxiety—he began a conscious search for order in his life. Finally, he had found a new source of direction and wholeness, only to discover that he had attained the status of an alien. This new awareness, unlike that which accompanied either form of anxiety, provided him with a sense of identity—a base line through

59

which to account for confusion and temptation in the world of the *saeculum.*

The *Confessions* represented Augustine's first major attempt to integrate the philosophical and psychological insights of his conversion with the years of study immediately preceding and following the conversion. As has been suggested, he approached this work with a keen sense of his audience, and the difficulties it faced in fourth-century Roman North Africa. He engaged his reader in a demanding psychological struggle that kept the edifying mission of his work always in the forefront. One must not, however, forget that the backdrop for this discussion of everyday problems was a profound religious vision and a sensitive philosophical insight. Augustine's tactics and strategy grew out of that vision—a vision of unity and perfection of God's truth—that made Augustine's own battles manageable, and that he had to represent to his parishioners, if he was to make theirs bearable. He sought always to mediate anxiety, to present to his reader a hint of the unity and order that he had found but could only approximate through his writing.[1]

Unity and Order

Augustine's attempt to communicate the latent unity and order in individuals and in social and political groups was vital to his entire endeavor—for those to whom he spoke had, he felt, lost a feeling for their own integrity and that of their social and political institutions. A kind of formal unity remained, but it had proven painfully inadequate. He hoped that he might communicate the possibility of unity, order, and integrity that was to be found in the world that they shared, so his readers might truly share that world.

Augustine's success in representing unity and order rested on his readers and his God. The argument made here is simply that in his own terms he had to make an attempt. If people were given access to or a hint of real perfection, the imperfection of their present lives would become more apparent. Furthermore, the universal perspective that he offered would, he felt, engage people in a regular confrontation with their imperfection—a confrontation that would have important psychological, political, as well as religious results. His was not a prophecy of doom, but rather a prophecy of qualified hope. To be frozen in despairing inaction by the power and perfection of his God would be to misunderstand the nature of God. Augustine's religion thus became the reverse of an "opiate": it was a call to action.

Augustine's concern with the problems of unity and order extends throughtout his *Confessions*. The unity and order to be found within each individual, and that between individuals, the unity of nature that was the result of God's design, the unity of the Scriptures, and the unity and totality that was God himself—each of these is addressed in the *Confessions*. All are brought together through Augustine's skilled craftsmanship in the composition of this work. From his earliest recognition of "that mysterious unity from whence I had my being" to a final insistence that "all bodies express this" order, Augustine is consistent.

> For a body which consists of members, all of which are beautiful, is by far more beautiful than the several members individually are, by whose well-ordered union the whole is completed, though these members also be severally beautiful.[2]

He hoped to strengthen and make beautiful individual parts of the soul and individuals in society, so human beings might more easily recognize their place in God's beautiful order. Once again, the *Confessions* is an important starting point in this endeavor.

Father Robert J. O'Connell has in fact suggested that a strict unity exists in the work.

> Augustine, Everyman, Adam. This secret identity governs the subtle development of the *Confessions,* harmonizes its themes, blends them into a symphonic unity, discloses their profoundest sense. A theory of man, indeed; man as Prodigal, lost sheep, soul in odyssey, peregrination, ambiguous term which can mean either "wandering" or "pilgrimage" depending on the direction of its movement, away from or back to God.[3]

It is this very concern with unity, O'Connell believes, that suggests an overarching unity to Augustine's work. He notes that Augustine's concern with oneness, growing out of his fascination with Neoplatonism, should alert the reader to seek for a unity in his writing.[4]

Father O'Connell's argument is convincing in many respects. It would be surprising, however, given Augustine's sophisticated understanding of his audience, if there were not in addition a unifying principle to be found within the parameters of the work itself. Another commentator has suggested, for example, that "one can legitimately prefer to see in the *Confessions* a unity *d'esprit* more internal than logical: a unity of spirit and intention more than a coherent ordering of developments."[5] In truth, the unity of Augustine's *Confessions* is both philosophic and passionate.

Augustine, through his *Confessions,* seeks to gain access to the wills of his readers and instruct them so that wills at variance with themselves become fixed upon one. At this moment "the whole united may be borne, which was before divided into many." It would now become possible for individuals, renewed and brought together, to act for the good of all. This was impossible before, he insists, until they faced the unity that was God. Individuals could not even recognize that which they shared, let alone act in defense of it. The aim of the *Confessions* in substance and form is to compel that confrontation with God and to elicit praise of god's unity.

Unity in Writing

What better way to praise God for all that He had done than to elicit praise from many others? What better way to show his appreciation than to instruct people in the skills of acting rightly? That Augustine's *Confessions* was crucial to this instruction, he tells us throughout, but most clearly at the end of Book IX. He asks there that he be allowed to offer this work in response to his mother's last request. She had asked that she be remembered by the prayers of others, and Augustine indicates that he in part responded to that request through writing the *Confessions.* This dedication is critical, for it introduces an additional source of thematic unity. Still, before returning to autobiographical problems and to Monnica's place in the entire work, we must examine more general structural problems, namely, the relation of the first nine autobiographical books to the final four.

Book X—The Power of Memory

The tenth book is far and away the easiest to integrate into the whole. It forms a transition between the autobiography of books one through nine and the scriptural exegesis of the last three. It introduces more explicitly the philosophical and theological underpinnings of the work, and yet subtly continues the emotion, even passion of the preceding books. Moreover, it introduces the problem of memory—only anecdotally hinted at before in an explicit and powerful discussion that is at the center of both his philosophic and psychological methods.

This book begins with Augustine personally confronting his audience, so they might remember the task that is theirs, even as he tells them again of his own responsibilities. He reminds them that they are witnesses to his written *Confessions*—his confession to God having been made silently.[6] He wonders why they should be more interested in his life than what they "themselves are?" The fruit to be reaped in his *Confessions* would be in its ability to move people from the dormancy of despair, awakening them to God's love and grace *"by which every weak person is made strong, who is by it made conscious of his own infirmity"* [7] (emphasis added).

The edifying mission extends that of the more directly autobiographical sections, but his argument has become more philosophical and more explicitly theological. Augustine's personality, his infirmities, and his strengths are still present, but they are more directly pointed at the end, rather than the path that is described in Books I through IX. He preaches now to "that brotherly mind" [8] that has been better prepared through his instruction. He had had to take his readers through an examination of the world of the flesh, before they could be introduced to the word of God and the scriptures.

Essentially, the tenth book is transitional, moving the readers beyond the example of Augustine, first to philosophical discussion and then—hopefully—to their own lives and histories. Eschewing direct spiritual exegesis, he continues to personalize and to remind his readers of what his "inner man" had come to know "by the ministry of the outer man." [9] In the same fashion, he reminds people of the limits of the outer man and his frequent inordinate love of material things. However important the things he learned from such objects, he wants to tell his reader that those who remained "subjects unto them" were not "fit to judge," precisely because they were subjects.[10] If unfit to judge, they could not in turn escape the prison of fools that they inhabited. To escape that prison, individuals must look into themselves for the edifying examples locked away in the "secret caves" [11] of their own memories.

The transitional character of the tenth book becomes apparent as Augustine begins a discussion of memory. From the beginning of Book I, it has been clear that memory is critical to Augustine's endeavor. But it is not until Book X—after his conversion, and perhaps most important, after the death of his mother has been reported—that the concept of memory receives a full treatment. Freed from the most burdensome of his own memories and aware of many of the secret caves in his being, Augustine can pass to a discussion of "the spacious places of [his] memory." [12] Moreover, now he can introduce his readers to the basis of the method that he has applied in the previous nine books, with some hope that they are now prepared for such metainstruction.

Memory was far more than mere mechanical recall for Augustine. It was a process of self-discovery—a means to that unity he had been denied as a youth. The involvement of the reader in the creative richness of Augustine's memory would, he hoped, suggest to that reader something of the subtle simplicity of the process. The search into the past was for a profound understanding of that which lay hidden below the conscious level.[13] The confessional method begins that search with the simple recall of past events, but it passes to the recollection of more fundamental states of human consciousness. When I am in the storehouse of memory, says Augustine,

> I demand that what I wish should be brought forth, and some things immediately appear; others require to be longer sought after, and are dragged, as it were, out of some hidden receptacle; others, again, hurry forth in crowds, and while another thing is sought and inquired for, they leap into view, as if to say, "is it not we, perchance?" Then I drive away with the hand of my heart from before the face of my remembrance, until what I wish be discovered making its appearance out of its secret cell. Other things suggest themselves without effort, and in continuous order, just as they are called for—those in front giving place to those that follow, and in giving place are treasured up again to be forthcoming when I wish it. All of which takes place when I repeat a thing from memory.[14]

A part of himself remained in the memory, he argued. To invoke the memory, to develop its power was—for Augustine—to begin the search for self. As the power of memory was awakened, it perceived that "its object of consideration was not as complete as usual, and, feeling the defect . . . it strove to get back what was missing." [15]

To remember to shout "This is it!" is, he suggests, not just to solve a problem, but the recognition that a part of something has been restored to a previously felt union. To find something in this sense is to remember that it once was. The examples are external and concrete. Like Plato, he found it difficult to talk directly of the psyche. Still the discussion is reminiscent of earlier references to his own wholeness.

The layers of memory, once penetrated and understood, connect to higher levels of knowledge. Augustine describes those facets of memory that recall the "four perturbations of the mind—desire, joy, fear and sorrow." [16] He passes to the more difficult notion that it is he himself with whom he meets in his memory. Only then can he speak of passing "beyond [his] memory" so that he can arrive at God.[17] Thus, he hopes to train his readers to look into their memories for evidence of God that he knew from experience would be difficult to discern.

He understood that his readers were still subject to pride and to those deceiving opinions upon which it fed. So long as they were, they could not be "joined . . . in any concord of charity but into the fellowship of punishment." [18] In style and substance, Book X indicates a shift in which the possibility of change is directly introduced, and the "power [of] the burden of custom to overload a man" [19] is recognized and set aside. Having carefully prepared his reader through the example of his own life, he could then turn to the example of Christ's life as the only true mediator between this world and the next, as the only true "remedy" for the soulful maladies of the earthly pilgrim. The reality of the Word made flesh was now made utterable. Augustine could then directly turn to that Word and an introductory lesson in reading the Scriptures.

Book XI—A Multiplicity of Times and a Unity of Purpose

The order of creation that Augustine perceives in Genesis is—he tells us—an order of times. It is an order that suggests by its very nature the possibility of disorder. God judges not "in relation to time, that which passes in time," he notes. His is an "ever-fixed eternity" that stands in contrast to the times of man, which appear to be constantly shifting and uncertain to the human creature, whose will constantly shifts as well.[20]

That order that his readers have begun to find in the recesses of their own memories is extended by dint of comparison to the order of God's creation. Still—despite his careful argumentation up to this point—Augustine cannot make this comparison immediately and directly. Again, he calls upon the spirit that has invaded his person to introduce his reader to the spirit that encompasses all.

The very idea of order is in fact introduced in the manner in which he has portrayed his life in his *Confessions.* "Why do I lay *in order* before [God] so many variations," he asks? Because it is very important to him "to be able to declare these things to [God] *in order*" and to make use of "the drops of time [which] are very precious with [him]." [21] All of this, in turn, is required so that he and his readers can better understand the scriptures and so that he can be "useful also to brotherly charity." [22] The order of God's creation, as presented by Moses, holds clues to all order—the order of the psyche, the order of the love of one human being for another in *caritas,* as well as the order of the scriptures themselves and the world that they describe. If people were to recognize that order, however, they would first have to understand the subtle temptation that was man's fascination with time.

Time limits the vision of human beings in at least two significant ways. First, it focuses attention on the motion of bodies, on discrete phenomena, which, by their multiplicity and diversity, turn our attention away from the possibility of unity and order in our own minds and in our world.[23] Second, it creates a fascination with things past and things future to the exclusion of the present and our duties to act in the present.[24] Time provides—he suggests—the boundaries within which our action takes place, and so it is necessary. Insofar as it moves beyond that boundary-setting function, however, it can inhibit human action in support of the whole—the "good of all." In the same way that the details of grammar had turned his attention from the purpose of an oration, so—he suggests—does time threaten to distract people "with tumultuous vicissitudes." [25] Dividing a person's life into fractions, these vicissitudes can blind him to the larger duty to discover the unity—personal and social—that is offered through Christian charity.

The power and significance of *memoria* was thus placed in perspective through the dimension of time. The turn inward "into the recesses of my memory," so necessary to self-understanding, was not sufficient. In looking at "the manifold rooms, wondrously full of multitudinous wealth" that was his memory, he was amazed, but was unable to find God or "to distinguish and to value everything according to its proper worth." [26]

Memory was an aid but—as complex and significant as it was—the act of remembering was but a means to an end. It had eventually to be surpassed.[27] The function of memory was not to praise nor criticize the past so much as it was to teach the individual who examined that past to overcome its distractions. Once again, Augustine was in search of the proper context in which the proper action—guided not by *cupiditas* but by *caritas*—could occur.

Book XII—An Ordered Truth in a Multiplicity of Opinions

The twelfth book is concerned with the nature of truth. From its initial warning about the difficulty of understanding the scriptures to its closing pleas for reading that scripture in the right spirit, it discusses the nature of a truth to be found in the order of human times. Here Augustine shifts his attention from man's relationship to God to man's knowledge of God through His scriptural messages. Augustine was careful here as always to mix, judiciously, warnings and cautions with the hope that there is something in the scriptures for everyone.

Of course Augustine understood that a diverse humanity could interpret the scriptures in different ways, But, clarity and simplicity could, he believed, emerge even out of a diversity of true opinions. It was more important to him that the end of "pure charity" should be addressed than it was for everyone to be in precise agreement about the meaning of scripture. There are, of course, true opinions, but Augustine is concerned that no one be overbearing in using them, lest "those 'little ones' who are living in hope" be terrified and retreat from them. What is most critical is that all be nourished so that "error not deceive us." [28]

His *Confessions* served as an interpretative guide through which one might avoid such deception, and so through which one might begin to understand himself—to act for himself and with his fellows to recreate a truly public existence that occurs only when the "good of all" is served to the "end of *caritas.*" He makes the parallel directly though humbly between his words and those of the scripture.

> Permit me, therefore, in these more briefly to confess unto Thee, and to select some one true certain and good sense, that Thou shalt inspire, although many senses offer themselves, where many indeed, may; this being the faith of my confession that if I should say that which Thy minister felt, rightly and profitably, this I should strive for.[29]

This plea in turn repeats his earnest hope that should he ever "write anything to have the highest authority," that he write it in such a way so as to "re-echo, rather than . . . [to] set down one true opinion so clearly on this as [to] exclude the rest." [30]

He implored people not to be confused by seeming contradiction, and to avoid an overly mechanical interpretation of the scriptures. The scriptures were neither a guidebook nor a simple message of logical and rational order. The truth of the scriptures was to be found in the *caritas* that they describe and espouse. The scriptures were to be held in common, but were of use only to those who used them lawfully "to the end of charity."

Book XIII—*The Peaceful Rest of* Caritatis Christi

Even in the final book that is the most concerned with matters of theology and scriptural exegesis, Augustine takes pains to integrate earlier themes into the whole work. There is in these discussions a hint of resolution of what before were confounding problems and difficulties. What had seemed nearly impossible in relation to Augustine's personal struggle, now began to seem manageable in relation to God's order and Christ's example. It had become less critical by the thirteenth book for him to note a child's dependence on God—a dependence that challenges "immoderate liberty" and beckons all into a new and easeful "unity." [31] The relationship between liberty and authority is made tenable in relation to the "eminent authority" [32] of the scriptures, and the power and limitation of human language is understood in relation to the limitless power of the word.

In all of Augustine's discussion in this book, there is the sense of an order and unity that is beyond our comprehension and thus beyond description in mere words.[33] Augustine suggests that the language he uses can only hint at that unity and order. He can speak of the Trinity as being represented in the human psyche and yet cannot so easily represent the Trinity that is God.[34] Likewise, he will use the story of creation as an elaborate allegory to remind his readers of the need to act righteously toward their neighbors, so they might catch a glimpse of that holy charity that is contained in the "knowledge of the love of Christ *(caritatis Christi)."* The end toward which Augustine aims is a complete beauty, which can be found only in the "whole."

And so must it be with Augustine's *Confessions,* with his readers, with the scriptures, and with God's creation. However beautiful a section of his writing, that section is fulfilled only in relation to the whole. However beautiful in faith and understanding one of his readers may be, that individual was all the more beautiful in relation to the whole of society. And so it was with the scriptures and with nature. If seen in relation to the whole—words and times, psyches and souls—the most pressing of human problems would be rendered tolerable or at least more tolerable than they had ever been.

In sum, the final book extends the notion of *caritas* to all that is good in God's creation and finally to that *peace* that allows the human race to surmount contention and strife.[35] He prays for a peace beyond human ordering, a peace portrayed—he suggests—in the first book of Genesis.

> But the seventh day is without evening, nor hath it any setting, because Thou hast sanctified it to an everlasting continuance; that that which Thou didst after Thy works, which were very good, resting on the seventh day, although in unbroken rest Thou madest them, that the voice of the Book may speak beforehand unto us, that we also after our work (therefore very good, because Thou hast given them to us) may repose in Thee also in the Sabbath of eternal life.[36]

This theme of peace is raised early in Book XIII and remains its central focus. Beginning with discussion of the peaceful rest that is the product of God's light,[37] he prays that he and his readers might attain "the peace of Jerusalem." [38] Insisting that contention and strife are inevitable without peace, that even the vision of unity is blocked without peace, Augustine prays for "the peace of quietness, the peace of the Sabbath, peace without any evening." [39] Any peace attainable in the *saeculum* is, of course, for Augustine but a pale reflection of eternal peace, yet even its approximation of true peace is useful to those who seek unity and truth both in this life and the next.

Apart from their common focus on Genesis, these last three books are linked as a special praise of God. In an Easter sermon to the people, Augustine spoke of the Ten Commandments and in particular of those three that refer to the love of God.

> The law moreover has ten precepts. The first precept of the law is that God alone, and no other is to be worshipped; no idol is to be made. The second precept is: "Thou shalt not take the name of God in vain!" The third precept is: Observe the sabbath day, not in an earthly manner . . . but spiritually. Those three precepts pertain to the love of God . . . because the Scripture says: Of these two commandments depend the whole Law and the Prophets, that is on the love of God and of the neighbor.[40]

Those three that pertain to the love of God he characterizes in the same sermon as representing "Unity, Truth and Peace." [41] Augustine has, it would seem, offered his own special praise of God through his writing of these last books of his *Confessions*. The unity, truth, and peace of which Augustine speaks in Books XI, XII, and XIII serve both as a lesson in scriptural exegesis and a teaching on the love of God. It remains to link these to the teachings of Books I through IX. The ninth book offers both structural and substantive clues to the unity of the whole.

Book IX—The Death of Monnica and the Resolution of Carnal Anxiety

The entire ninth book serves as a kind of review—a review that highlights even more directly than before the central position of his mother. In addition, it confirms a unity that involves the resolution of philosophical problems and personal crises.

Augustine had been converted, but had not yet been baptized as the book begins. There can be no doubt that Christianity was still a great mystery to him. Still, it had allowed him to begin to face the corruption of his youth, and to find a new strength with which to combat the lures of deceit and ambition. Friendship grew beyond youthful insecurity. The joy of common prayer had a healing power beyond previous imagination. Distress, once caused by the possessive search for friendship, was cured through the brotherhood of a common search for God.

Still, he was not ready to comprehend fully the nature of his conversion. His baptism only sets the stage for further understanding. It was only with the death of his mother that some resolution began.

The praise of Monnica in Book IX, Chapter IX is striking, for it has been clear from the beginning that Augustine's feelings about her were ambivalent. Her role in his final decision was, of course, prominent, but her method of influence was questioned by Augustine, Ambrose, and others. The nature of her ambition for him was at odds with the aim of her striving. The result of her pushing was clearly rebellion!

Through his conversion, she was rewarded to a far greater extent, he says, "than she used to ask by her pitiful and most doleful groanings." Both mother and son had learned much from their trials, and both were rewarded. Only in Chapter X of Book IX could Augustine begin to work out what remained the most difficult of his carnal tensions. It is significant that this should occur not only after his conversion, but as her last days approached.

> As the day now approached on which she was to depart this life (which day Thou knewest, we did not), it fell out—Thou, as I believe, by Thy secret ways arranging it—that she and I stood alone, leaning in a certain window, from which the garden of the house we occupied at Ostia could be seen; at this place, *removed from the crowd;* we were *resting* ourselves for the voyage, after the fatigue of a long journey. We then were conversing alone very pleasantly; and *forgetting* those things which are behind, and reaching for unto those things which are before, we were seeking between ourselves in the presence of the Truth. . . .[42]

The scene is thus set apart from the pressure of the crowd, its love of error and its whimsically shifting opinions. No longer involved in the fast pace of Roman life, they permitted themselves the luxury of forgetting the past—both their own and that of the Roman culture that had imprisoned them both. The long journey that precedes this moment is, of course, crucial. The difficulty and the pain of that journey have, however, been both necessary and worthwhile. It appears that they can now pass beyond memory and begin to explore the truth. Augustine continues.

> And when our conversation had arrived at that point, that the very *highest pleasure of carnal senses,* and that the *very brightest material light,* seemed by reason of the sweetness of that life not only not worthy of comparison, but not even of mention, we lifting ourselves . . . did *gradually pass through all corporeal things,* and . . . *we came to our own minds, and went beyond them,* that we might advance as high as that region of unfailing plenty, where Thou feedest Israel forever with the food of Truth, and where *life is that Wisdom* by whom all these things are made. . . . And while we were thus speaking, and straining after her, we slightly touched her with the whole effort of our heart; and we sighed, and there left bound the first fruits of the Spirit; and *returned to the noise of our own mouth, where the word uttered has both beginning and end.* And what is like unto Thy Word, our Lord, who remaineth in Himself without becoming old, and *maketh all things new?*[43] (emphasis added).

Overcoming the chains of existence required that they first pass through the carnal and material essences of this life. Only then could they pass beyond the distractions and distortions of people, things, and times, and enter a place where one had *only to be*. Still, even here the release could not be complete. God's word was blurred by the "noise of our own mouth," returning the pair to the world of times of men, but leaving them with the promise of hope that all things might be made new. That promise could not be fulfilled in this life, but would positively affect one's ability to survive in this world.

The experience of his mother's death forced Augustine to grow beyond customary habits and sentiments to a higher love of both God and mortals. To do this, he had to understand his mother in relation to God—along with her inevitable role in his relationship to God. Confronted with his mother's dead body, he had been unable to cry. He consciously wrestled with ancient psychological reactions, but was unable to express his grief freely. "I knew what I repressed in my heart"—he said—"And I was exceedingly annoyed that these human things had such power over me. . . ." [44] He could not express his feelings, until he began to recall Ambrose's hymn of praise. Only in the remembrance of God would he bring back thoughts of his mother as a devout worshipper.

> Then, by degrees, I recovered my former way of thinking of Thy handmaiden and her holy behavior in regard to Thee, along with her saintly kindness and benevolence toward us, of which I was suddenly bereft. It was a relief to weep in Thy sight about her and for her, about myself and for myself.[45]

Only now could he forget these things that were behind, and praise her life with his tears. He had for this moment resolved the unresolvable and overcome the "due order of destiny of our natural condition." [46] He had not escaped his carnal affections, but he had more clearly come to understand their hold. This was clearly a break more profound than that accomplished in his conversion.

Monnica, therefore, became a kind of mediator herself. As the *Confessions* was in some ways a mediator between his readers and the scriptures, so Monnica served as a real, human, and emotional mediator between the carnal and the spiritual in Augustine's life. The tensions felt between Augustine and his mother were real. They were overcome only in death, but the course of their resolution—Augustine hoped—provided valuable insight to him who would carefully consider his plea. This is apparent in the conclusion of Book IX. Common prayer for Monnica and an understanding of her complexities might open his brethren—his fellow pilgrims—to new possibilities for their own interactions.

> . . . . that so what my mother in her last words desired of me, may be *fulfilled* for her in the prayers of many, *more plentifully through my Confessions than through my prayers* [47] (emphasis added).

Augustine suggests in these significant passages the basis for the thematic unity of the entire work. "The mother of us all" stands out sharply against Augustine's "Catholic Mother," [48] as he shifted to a new and continuing familial relationship in the church. His mention of "Jerusalem my mother" redirects attention to Monnica, but also beyond her, and so is preparatory for the final four books.

> And I will not be turned away until Thou collect all that I am from this dispersion and deformity, into the peace of that very dear mother, where are the first fruites of my spirit, whence these things are issued to me, and Thou conform and confirm it forever, my God, my mercy.[49]

Likewise references to "our mother charity" seem in context to be carefully considered. They appear to be designed to keep alive the ninth book in the mind of his reader and so maintain an awareness of the sort of personal changes that were introduced there. The ninth and tenth books prepare the reader for the unity, truth, and peace that follow. The ninth, in its summary resolution of earlier crises associated with the carnal senses and material light opens the way for a new kind of wisdom. The ninth book is, in addition, symbolic of the resolution of all carnal anxiety and the basis of a structural unity that grows out of Augustine's fascination with classical arithmology.

Unity in Number

Augustine's own words and the arrangements of the parts of the whole that is the *Confessions* provide evidence of the importance of number to him.[50] Though God is without number, Augustine claimed, numbering was very important to him in this his praise of God. "Whatsoever good I have learned," he prays, "unto Thy service let it be directed, yea whatsoever I speak, or write or number, let it all serve Thee." [51] A discussion of scriptural numbers in *De Trinitate*—written in about 400 A.D., and so very near the time of the writing of his *Confessions*—confirms the importance of arithmology for his study of the

Word. In the midst of an inquiry into the significance of specific numbers in the scriptures, he remarks:

> As to the reasons, indeed, why these numbers are so put into the Holy Scriptures, other people may trace out other reasons, either such that those which I have given are to be preferred to them, or such as are equally probable with mine, or even more probable than they are; *but there is no one surely so foolish or so absurd as to contend that they are so put in the Scriptures for no purpose at all, and that there are no mystical reasons why those numbers are there mentioned* [52] (emphasis added).

Given his clearly stated intention to imitate to the best of his ability the style and substance of the scriptures, it would be surprising indeed if Augustine's own use of numbers were put there for no purpose at all. On the contrary, he seems to have made careful use of numbers in his ordering of the *Confessions,* and in particular in his writing of the ninth book.

Augustine's biblical scholarship led him to place a special significance on the number nine. He described the death of Christ, for example, in the following passage in *De Trinitate:*

> For He was crucified first by the cross of the Jews at the third hour . . . then he was suspended by the cross itself at the sixth hour, and gave up his spirit at the ninth hour.[53]

This passage that is a part of the same discussion of scriptural numbers noted above is particularly interesting in light of Augustine's use of the number nine in his *Confessions,* where he mentions it on four occasions. On the first three occasions, he refers to his nine years as a Manichean,[54] during which his mother waited patiently until he became ripe for instruction.[55] He seduced himself and others in public for nine years "by those arts that are called liberal, but in private [he] still pretended the assumed name of religion"—Manicheanism.[56] The fourth use of the number nine comes in the ninth book as he describes the death of his mother "in the ninth day . . . of her sickness." [57] In each of the four cases, he directs attention to a period of suffering, and more particularly, to the end of suffering—an end that Christ found at the ninth hour on the cross. In each case—after nine years, nine days, and nine hours—there was liberation. Christ's death was, for Augustine, of special importance because it taught people how to live in *caritas* and liberated them from some of their earthly, carnal bonds. In Augustine's terms, Monnica's death was liberating for her. There is, furthermore, the suggestion that it was liberating for Augustine as well, and surely after nine years of suffering, he, Augustine, had found a new and easeful freedom. It was only after her death that he began his search in earnest—freed from his strongest remaining carnal affection.

The ninth book thus becomes both the literal and figurative focus of the whole *Confessions*. Not only does it resolve many of the carnal anxieties that have been introduced before, but it introduces—through the symbolism associated with the number nine—the final resolution of all carnal anxiety that came with Christ's sacrifice. In addition, this book prepared the way for all that follows. Indeed the last four chapters of Book IX introduce themes more fully discussed in the correspondingly numbered books that follow.

The problems introduced by Augustine and his mother in their conversation at Ostia in Chapter X, Book IX are clarified in his elaborate discussion of memory in the tenth book.

> So great is the power of memory, so great the power of life in man, whose life is mortal. What then shall I do, O Thou my true life, my God? I will pass beyond this power of mine which is called memory—I will pass beyond it that I may proceed to Thee, O Thou sweet Light. What says Thou to me? Behold, I am soaring by my mind towards Thee who remainest above me. I will also pass beyond this power of mine which is called memory, wishful to reach Thee whence Thou canst be reached, and to cleave unto Thee whence it is possible to cleave unto Thee.[58]

The skill of forgetting was learned only slowly and only after he had first remembered. The burden of habit had first to be recognized—only then could it be avoided. Augustine develops insight in Book X in a discussion that is less a resolution than an elaboration of an experience that he had portrayed in Chapter X of Book IX. His mother's guidance thus is shown to have opened for him the possibility of a new richness—at that time still undiscovered. A new mediator would be found in the tenth book with the suggestion of a new way to approach "that moment of knowledge" that he had found at Ostia with his mother. For in Him, says Augustine, in the last chapter of Book X, "are hid all the treasures of wisdom and knowledge." [59] The tenth book becomes the capstone of the tenth chapter of the ninth book. The wisdom associated in Augustine's mind with the number ten followed the ninth hour of his mother's life, the nine days of her final illness, and the nine years of her waiting for her son to become teachable.

Likewise, the eleventh book's concern with time and unity helps to explain Monnica's decision—in Chapter XI of Book IX—not to be buried with her husband Patricius. She had originally asked to be buried next to him so

> that this should be added to that happiness, and be talked of among men, that after her wandering beyond the sea, it had been granted her that they both, so united on earth, should lie in the same grave.[60]

She overcame this need, however, when she began to understand more fully those things divine and to compare such needs to the unity that was God. The false unity of spatial closeness was no longer so important. A new understanding of unity—spatial and temporal—had begun to displace an earlier and more conventional one.

This was, however, a truth that came only slowly to her son. Only after having remembered the words of Ambrose's hymn, could he begin to focus on that most difficult truth—that there was something beyond the shape and form of this world to which his mother belonged.[61] In approaching truth in Book XII, he attempts to open for himself and his audience a way to ease such difficulty as he had encountered. He introduces the truth of the scriptures so it will be available to all. The scriptures will, in turn, offer to those who accept it instruction that will aid them in times of need, such as that expressed by Augustine in Chapter XII of Book IX.

In the course of time they too might—he suggests in Book XIII—be inflamed and born upwards. No one without peace sees that vision, he says, of God's unity and truth.[62] Monnica had come close to peace and offered her son at Ostia a vision that he in turn sought to share with others.

The thirteen chapters of the ninth book of the *Confessions* offer both a summary and a sense of direction that brings unity to the thirteen books of the entire work. Perhaps more importantly, they lend understanding to a discussion that passes on many levels at once. They unite the passionate and the philosophic, the personal and the more general instructive missions of Augustine. He seems to say in the ninth book: If you, reader, understand Monnica and me, you will understand something very important about yourself. If, however, you are truly to understand us, you must look beyond the narrative of our relationship as it appears in the first nine books. You must look as well to the philosophic and religious teaching that begins in those books and is developed more completely in the final four. Carnal affections and material delights, he hints, cannot be explained on their own terms. They will be really understood only if seen in dramatic contrast to the spiritual and eternal perspective that is God. But again, Augustine's genius is to have understood that the spiritual and eternal had to be introduced slowly and subtly. They could not be presented until people had begun to remember those facets of their lives that seemed useless in a Roman world. Augustine's "faculty of expression" and his "manner of composing" were meant to evoke those memories. All that he writes and numbers in this work were as well in the service of God and directed toward the end of awakening in his readers a new sense of hope.

Through his numbering, Augustine attempted to express the otherwise inexpressable. He could, through his ordered and careful work, praise God for those things that his heart was unable to express, and at the same time offer an example of what the scriptures do on another level. Here Augustine expressed not perfection but the road to perfection through self-understanding in the love of God.

Though God be without number, Augustine argued, He had ordered all things in measure, number, and weight.[63] Though Augustine did not presume a divine mission parallel to that of Moses, he surely longed for a *faculty of expression* and a *manner of composing* that might bring honor both to his mother and to his God. The unity and order of his praise was significant only as it encouraged people to discover the potential for unity and order—social and psychological—that had been lost in their privatized worlds. The proper understanding and use of memory and time would, he believed, allow people to confront the truth and catch a glimpse of peace and that unity and order attendant to it.

A further detailed explication of an arithmological code as the basis of the unity of the *Confessions* would almost surely lose that sense of wholeness and community for which Augustine strove throughout this work and throughout his life. In fact, the structure of the *Confessions* is significant only insofar as it symbolically expressed the pathos of earthly suffering and the glory of salvation.

Though salvation could not be willfully obtained by anyone, Augustine believed that his instruction could bear fruit in the relations of his readers—one to another. They could, he believed, be taught to understand more clearly the nature of their suffering, and learn thereby to act more forcefully in pursuit of *caritas*. Eventually, he hoped, an alternative to the order that was Rome could be built. Roman politics and society, he would later argue, were based not on *caritas* but on *cupiditas*. His task in his *Confessions,* in structure and in theme, was to expose the dominance of *cupiditas* and to prepare the way for an understanding and acceptance of *caritas* as the foundation of a new and more lasting society.

Notes

1. *St. Augustine's Confessions,* 2 vols., The Loeb Classical Library, 1912, I, 1. *(Confs.)*
2. *Confs.,* XII, 20. See *Nicene and Post Nicene Fathers,* vol. IV, p. 352.

    For we Catholic Christians worship God, from whom are all good things whether great or small; from whom is all measure great or small; from whom is all form great or small; from whom is all order great or small. For all things in proportion as they are better measured, formed, and ordered, are assuredly good in a higher degree; but in proportion as they are measured, formed, and ordered in an inferior degree, are they the less good. These three things, therefore, measure, form, and order,— not to speak of innumerable other things that are shown to pertain to these three,—these three things, therefore, measure, form, order, are as it were generic goods in things made by God, whether in spirit or in body. God is, therefore, above every measure of the creature, above every form, above every order, nor is He above by local spaces, but by ineffable and singular potency, from whom is every measure, every form, every order. These three things, where they are great, are great goods, where they are small, are small goods; where they are absent, there is no good. And again where these things are great, there are great natures, where they are small, there are small natures, where they are absent, there is no nature.

3. Robert J. O'Connell, *Saint Augustine's Confessions: The Odyssey of the Soul,* Harvard University Press, Cambridge, 1969, p. 186. (O'Connell)
4. Ibid., p. 11ff.
5. A. Solignac, "Introduction" to *Les Confessions,* Oeuvres St. Augustin, Traduction de E. Tré Lorel et G. Boissou, Desclée de Brower, 1962, vol. 13, p. 20. (Solignac)
6. *Confs.,* X, 2.
7. Ibid., X, 3.
8. Ibid., X, 4.
9. Ibid., X, 6.
10. Ibid.
11. Ibid., X, 10.
12. Ibid., X, 8.
13. See, for example, *De Trinitate,* XI 3-4, *Nicene and Post Nicene Fathers,* vol. III, pp. 147-48 (hereafter cited as *De Trinitate.)*
14. *Confs.,* X, 8.
15. *Confs.,* X, 19.
16. *Confs.,* X, 14.
17. *Confs.,* X, 17.
18. *Confs.,* X, 36.
19. *Confs.,* X, 40.
20. *Confs.,* XI, 1.
21. *Confs.,* XI, 2.
22. Ibid.
23. Ibid., XI, 24.
24. See *Confs.,* XI, 14ff.

25. *Confs.*, XI, 29.
26. Ibid., X, 40.
27. Ibid., X, 17. But see also *Confs.*, XI, 29, where Augustine speaks of "stretching forth not to what shall be and shall pass away, but to those things which are before . . . for the garland of my heavenly calling. . . ." He suggests here that the best way to overcome the distractions of time is to keep one's attention fixed on the truth and order of God.
28. Ibid., XII, 30.
29. Ibid., XII, 32.
30. Ibid., XII, 31.
31. Ibid., XIII, 2; see also XIII, 7–8.
32. Ibid., XIII, 15.
33. Ibid., XIII, 7 and 38.
34. Ibid., XIII, 11.
35. Ibid.
36. Ibid., XIII, 35–36.
37. Ibid., XIII, 3, 8.
38. Ibid., XIII, 9.
39. Ibid., XIII, 35.
40. *Sermons,* Migne, vol. 44, 1165–66.
41. Ibid.
42. Ibid., IX, 10. The dramatic force of this exchange warrants detailed examination both as an indication of the newly found spiritual capacities of Augustine and his mother, and as a summary of the major themes of his autobiography.
43. Ibid.
44. Ibid., IX, 12.
45. Ibid.
46. Ibid.
47. Ibid., IX, 13.
48. Ibid., XII, 16.
49. Ibid.
50. F. E. Cranz has suggested that by the time of the *Confessions,* Augustine had sharply changed his earlier notions that claimed the existence of "immutable numbers which exist in immutable truth itself." Cranz is correct in noting the significance of the introductory psalm in this respect. The first sentence of the *Confessions* does in fact introduce the problem of number, as Augustine says, "great art Thou, O Lord, and greatly to be praised; great is Thy power and of Thy wisdom there is no number." Cranz would have done well, however, to look carefully to other discussions of number in the *Confessions* and elsewhere. In fact the idea of "number" remains central to Augustine's thinking in sermons and letters as well as in more formal work. (F. E. Cranz, "The Development of Augustine's Ideas on Society before the Donatist Controversy," in *Augustine: A Collection of Critical Essays,* R. A. Marcus, editor, Anchor Books, New York, 1972, p. 360ff.)
51. *Confs.*, I, 15.
52. *De Trinitate,* IV, 6.10, *Nicene and Post Nicene Fathers,* vol. III, p. 75.
53. Ibid.
54. *Confs.*, III, 11, 12.

55. *Confs.,* III, 12
56. *Confs.,* V, 6. Also see IV, 1.
57. *Confs.,* IX, 11.
58. *Confs.,* X, 17.
59. Ibid., IX, 10.
60. Ibid., IX, 11.
61. Ibid., IX, 12.
62. Ibid., IX, 13.
63. Ibid., I, 12.

CHAPTER 4

Caritas: The Ultimate and the Proximate End

This is the love that renews us, making us new men, heirs of the New Testament, singers of the new song. It was this love, brethren beloved that renewed also those of olden time, who were then the righteous, the patriarchs and prophets, as it did afterwards the blessed apostles: it is it, too, that is now renewing nations. . . .

Tractates on the Gospel of St. John, LXV, 1

The last three chapters have considered Augustine's use of the confessional method towards the end of Christian charity. Christian instruction was for Augustine more than contemplation of a future world of Christian fraternity. It was also a guide for people in the pursuit of *caritas* within the context of this life. In this chapter, we must look more closely at the meaning of *caritas* and its significance for Augustine's social and political thought.

The aim of the teacher is to unite the congregation "through the bond of love," thereby providing an example of, and a foundation for, the further development of true friendship. This unity might also reflect a sense of the public virtue to be found in the Christian community. Augustine had not found such public virtue in either Roman practice or in Roman philosophy, as he noted in a letter written in 412 A.D.

What discourses or writings of philosophers, what laws of any commonwealth in any land or age, are worthy for a moment to be compared with

> the two commandments on which Christ saith that all the law and the
> prophets hang: "Thou shalt love the Lord thy God with all thy heart,
> and with all thy soul, and with all thy mind, and thou shalt love thy
> neighbor as thyself?" [1]

Augustine came to see *caritas* as both the source of political morality
and the heart of true philosophy. *Caritas* for Augustine is the opposite
of *cupiditas*. The affection of *caritas* promotes unity and harmony.
Whereas, the passionate longing of *cupiditas* promotes disunity and
confusion. *Cupiditas* is a bad love in that it consumes all that it touches,
possessively denying the individuality and integrity of other people,
and fearfully and enviously holding on to material possessions. It is
divisive because it never allows people to develop those genuine bonds
of affection that flow from reciprocal commitment. It is privatizing because it promotes the jealous defense of material possessions. *Caritas*—
in every respect—reverses the tendencies of *cupiditas*.

Caritas demands autonomy in that it is a love that must be freely
and unconditionally given. It must permit an evergrowing commitment
to other people. It is dedicated to the good of all, to the common weal.
A good love, *caritas*

> was accorded its due importance so that men, for whom harmony was
> useful and honorable, might be bound by ties of various relationships in
> his one self but that these connections should be severally distributed
> among individuals and in this way serve to weld social life more securely
> by covering in their multiplicity a multiplicity of people.[2]

There are, however, at least two general problems that Augustine
faced in talking about *caritas*. One is common to much of his writing
and has been discussed above—the problem of the limitations of language in describing something that in its ultimate form is *amor Dei*.
This was a problem that called forth many of Augustine's skills as a
teacher, preacher, and scholar. Here as before, his attempt to overcome
these limitations—or at the least to deal with the problems within the
limits which they impose—is crucial.

The inexpressibility of *caritas* presents the first problem for Christian
instruction, but the nature of love more broadly considered creates a
second. Love can have many objects, he insisted. People are propelled
by their loves according to the nature of those objects. As one commentator notes:

> Love is desire and longing whether it is directed to temporal things or to
> God and the eternal. For Augustine love is a longing indifferent in itself,

whose quality is determined by the object to which it is directed. It can
be the highest—but it can be the lowest. . . . Love is the elementary
motive power in all human action, good and bad alike.[3]

Obviously, then, it was vital to Augustine's search for excellence to
prevent a confusion between *caritas* and its possessive counterfeit,
cupiditas. As he suggests in his *Confessions,* "The enticements of the
wanton would fain be deemed love; and yet is naught more enticing
than Thy charity. . . ." [4] The danger of confusion was real. It had
diverted the young Augustine. He hoped that he could expose the nature of that diversion to others.

Self-Love, Friendship, and Community

In order to cope with the confusion introduced by desire, Augustine
discussed the relationship of *caritas* to self-love, friendship, and community. He knew, of course, that each could be grounded in *cupiditas,*
but he insisted that each is fulfilled only if it rests upon *caritas.* Self-
love would have to be carefully ordered, he warned, if it was to avoid
greed and so begin to serve *caritas.* Friendship could likewise be con-
sumed by possessiveness and selfish jealousy. People were bound together in societies in many different ways—again according to the
objects of their affection. He hoped that people could discover and
learn to cherish civic bonds other than the power and greed that defined the Roman commonwealth.

Self-Love: Neutral, Inordinate, and Ordinate

As was the case in his *Confessions,* Augustine began his instruction in
caritas with the self—his own and that of his reader or listener. He
sought an ordered estimate of self, a self-love that loves "not more our
own private good than Thee, the good of all." [5] As John Burnaby
among others has noted, Augustine distinguished at least three sorts of
self-love.[6] The first was little more than an instinct to self-preservation.
As he suggests in the *City of God,* it is a natural feeling that a man
cherish himself and so avoid death.[7] It is a feeling that is critical and
inevitable, but it alone could not create the ordered self-love that
would lead people to confront life rather than to escape it. This sort of
self-love was morally neutral.

A second kind of self-love seeks to deny dependence through the
domination of personal preeminence. Pride and envy are the driving
forces of this sort of love. It is a love that consumes. One that loves in

this way loves so that others "may cease to be." He loves so that "he may make away with them." [8] This love looks only to self-aggrandizement, not to an enduring and reciprocal love of another, and surely, Augustine argued, not to the true advantage of the self. But this dangerous sort of self-love went even further than the love of money, of which the Apostle Timothy warned. It is, Augustine noted, most aptly labeled avarice, but a general avarice that goes beyond that love of money and "makes a man seek for something more than is fitting, for the sake of his own preeminence and through a kind of love of possession. Such love is well called 'private,' for all 'privation is a vanishing': it reduces, not enlarges the self." "When a man is too well pleased with himself," suggested Augustine, he would inevitably fail to take note of those around him.[9]

A third kind of love is ordered and just, says Augustine in *On Christian Doctrine:*

> He lives in justice and sanctity who is an unprejudiced assessor of the intrinsic value of things. He is a man who has an *ordinate love:* he neither loves what should not be loved nor fails to love what should be loved. . . .[10]

This ordinate love is characteristic of one who has been taught and taught carefully to love himself. A just man must learn "the fiction of being content with his own resources" and know also to use those resources well.[11] Ordinate self-love is inextricably tied to a man's love of God and of his fellows.

> The love wherewith a man truly loves himself is none other than the love of God. For he who loves himself in any other way is rather to be said to hate himself; since he becomes evil and loses the light of righteousness, when he turns aside from the higher and more excellent good to himself—a conversion which needs bring him to what is lower and poorer.[12]

The problem—as always for Augustine—was how to achieve this estimable goal.[13]

The instructional pattern is, in fact, very similar to his discussion of the unity of the self in his *Confessions.* Individual self-love *(Amor sui usque ad contemptum Dei)* promotes arrogant claims to knowledge and power *(Amor suae potestatis).* More profoundly, it fails to contain a perverse will *(voluntas perversa)* that instead fluorishes as a "love of personal preeminence" *(Amor excellentiae propriae).*

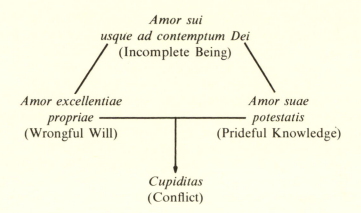

Caritas surely cannot triumph over conflict in a world in which arrogance and intellectual pride join in a mock battle with the desire for personal preeminence. An individual must remain incomplete in this situation, for he is dependent on ever-changing norms and opinions for his sense of self. It is only when *amor sui* is clearly subordinated to *amor Dei* that it can begin to serve *caritas* by promoting humility and a right will.

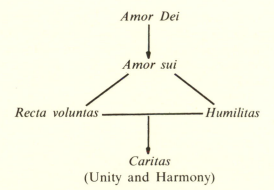

Caritas thus offers support for both self-love and the love of God. It serves the immediate goals of human action in the *saeculum* as well as the more distant goal of eternal peace.

Friendship—The Beginning of Neighborly Love

The challenge for human friendship, and ultimately for community, was great. One could love another as an exclusive possession, thus objectifying him and building an implicit barrier that limits the growth of that relationship and surely forestalls the development of the more inclusive relationships of community. Alternatively, one could share with him a love held in common; in Augustine's terms, a common quest.

Augustine's brief but highly dramatic study of friendship in his *Confessions* speaks to the dangers of an all-consuming relationship. In a scene discussed above, he recounts his reaction to a dying friend.

> Immediately, as soon as I was able to speak to him (and I could as soon as he was able, for I did not leave him, since *we were too dependent on each other),* I tried to make a joke with him, as if he, too, would laugh along with me at the baptism which he had received when completely out of his mind and senses. However, he had already learned that he had received it. And he was as much in horror of me as of an enemy, and warned me, with amazing and sudden *independence* of mind, that I had to stop saying such things if I desired to remain his friend. Dumbfounded and disturbed, I repressed all my feelings so that he might first grow well and be in such condition of health that I could deal with him as I wished [14] (emphasis added).

He soon lost his friend and reports that life became unbearable to one who would not love "as a half-being." For Augustine, notes John Burnaby, "the real inhumanity is to love a human being . . . not for what is 'common' but for what is 'private' . . . ." [15] Augustine lacked the strength and independence that his dying friend had found. He had failed at this moment to recognize that a true friendship was reliant on the independence of each friend.

Augustine felt that "a man becomes like the object he loves" and that many available "objects" could be possessed exclusively. Indeed, he notes that "Covetousness desires to possess much. . . ," but fear of losing these exclusive possessions entrapped people in a privatized world, for it was a fear that is concerned primarily with its own security.[16] Envy, omnipresent in a society that cherishes status and possessions, can aggravate this isolation all the more. Augustine, of course, attacked the isolation falsely imposed by the conventions of this world. Though it was for him a world in which people were and had to remain fundamentally alienated from the good life and from a true *patria,* it makes no sense, he argued, to cut oneself off even more completely.

The independence and strength for which Augustine strove will have been accomplished when the will serves the good of all by clinging to "immutable good." [17] Those who lacked such independence would require careful training of the sort that he had experienced. It would be a slow and gradual training that encountered carnal and material things first, and only then moved to the spiritual. The uninitiated would have to drink milk and see by the light of the moon before he could eat meat and enjoy the dazzling light of the sun.

> For it is the office of a wise training to bring one near to [Wisdom] in a certain graduated approach, but to arrive in her presence without these intermediate steps is a scarcely credible felicity.[18]

The Good of All—Extending the Love of Neighbor

Augustine sought to distinguish between private and public worlds so that he might create a place for the latter. Truth is something, he says, which is and must be shared.

> You do not turn anything to your private advantage by communion with truth. Whatever you may take from truth and wisdom, they still remain complete for me. I need not wait for you to return the source of your inspiration in order that I can be inspired by the truth. No part of the truth is ever made the private property of anyone. . . .[19]

Truth thus offered a way to Christian community or at least the best approximation of community available to men in the *saeculum*.

Augustine, like Plato, was concerned with building community—a community composed of strong individuals. His discussion of the nature of a people is in many ways parallel to that of Plato. A people, he argued in the *City of God*, is determined by the objects of its love. In examining those objects, we might be able to realize that truly common object that could become the foundation of a peace and order that might be more enduring and more just. Like Socrates, he hopes to discover the nature of a healthy city through an examination of the education of its citizens. He hoped to create a new foundation for social interaction from which might emanate that common love that determines the character of any association.

Thus, Augustine offered social training that would leave each individual able to judge matters of this life more independently and effectively—training that would create a group capable of supporting and defending that independence, physically and psychologically. The love of neighbor would pay immediate rewards, Augustine suggested. These rewards would, he hoped, lead to a better understanding both of self and neighbor through a more explicit confrontation with the love of God. Augustine describes a part of this process in his commentary on the Gospel of St. John.

> Begin, then, to love thy neighbor. "Break thy bread to the hungry, and bring into thy house him that is needy without shelter; if thou seest the

> naked, clothe him; and despise not those of the household of thy
> seed. . . ." Then shall thy light break forth as the morning light." Because
> He shall come to thee after the night of this world.[20]

"The love of neighbor comes first" and prepares the way for the love
of God that in turn strengthens the individual by making ordinate self-
love more possible. Having been thus strengthened, the individual is
more free to engage in truly reciprocal relations of affection with
friends and neighbors. This individual may not yet fully appreciate the
joy to be found in the love of God, but his appreciation of the power
of that love grows with the realization that he lives more easily and
comfortably with his neighbors, and he becomes stronger and more
independent though his ordinate self-love.

The process is one that proceeds from the social to the personal and
back to the social again. First, entering into association with his fellows,
the individual becomes more secure in himself and more aware of both
his responsibilities to others and of the aid that others can give to
him.[21] Then, examining the source of his newfound solace and comfort,
he discovers that "God is love and he that dwelleth in love dwelleth in
God." [22] His personal commitment to God's law thus reinforced,
he turns back to his friends and neighbors and the society they share
with an ever more powerful commitment to that society and those
neighbors.

But this process of social training was only the foundation of Augustine's instruction in *caritas,* and on the principles of public virtue
through which civic bonds and the standards of excellence that govern
nations emerge. Speaking again in his commentary, "On the Gospel of
St. John," he notes that:

> This is the love that *renews us,* making us new men, heirs of the New
> Testament, singers of the new song. It was this love, brethren beloved,
> that *renewed also those of olden time,* who were then the righteous, the
> patriarchs and prophets, as it did afterwards the blessed apostles: *it is it,*
> *too, that is now renewing nations* . . .[23] (emphasis added).

His goal is clear—the creation of a society the members of which "have
a mutual interest in one another [so that] if one member suffers, all the
members suffer; and one member honored, all the members rejoice
with it." [24]

At times, Augustine seems to be speaking of a universal Christian
community, but at others it is clear that he hopes that the principles of
Christian community will affect existing nations and human institutions. The love of which he speaks is, he notes, the basis of all virtue—

"joy, peace, long-suffering, kindness, goodness, faith, meekness and temperance." Furthermore, it endorses and encompasses the classical Roman virtues, "the prevalence of which in any city entitles it to be spoken of as fluorishing." Without this love, he insists, "all good things can be of no avail." [25] This, he suggests, is true for the earthly city as well as for the heavenly. Writing to Nectarius in 408 A.D., he advises that,

> the greater is your desire to leave your country in a safe and flourishing condition, [the more he should take Christianity seriously]. Away with all these vanities and follies, and let men be converted to the true worship of God, and to chaste and pious manners: *then will you see your country fluorishing,* not in the vain opinion of fools, but *in the sound judgment of the wise.* . . . We are, therefore, resolved, neither on the one hand to lay aside Christian gentleness, nor on the other side to leave in your city that which would be a most pernicious example for all others to follow [26] (emphasis added).

The Power of Love

Love as Desire and Yearning

John Burnaby in his comprehensive study of *caritas—Amor Dei—*suggests that "The power of love to call forth love is seen alike in sensual passion and in pure friendship." Augustine, speaking to the people, extends this observation, describing the consequences of an impure love on the one hand and a holy love on the other. He contrasts impure love with holy love. "Impure love leads to a lust for passing, temporal things. Holy love raises us to heavenly things and inflames us with what is eternal." Love in general, he insists, has a power of its own that cannot be denied by the lover. The virtue attached to the power of love depends, therefore, on the way in which it is used.[27]

The problem, then, is not so much in getting people in motion. People will always seek their own good, and will always be propelled toward that which they see as their good by the power of love, Augustine says. All desire a happy life but where, he inquires, are they to find knowledge of it? People may seek the good life in places where it cannot be found. Though people want to be happy, they will, he warns, often fail to understand the nature of happiness—their own and that of others. A happy man, he suggests, must not only have all that he wants, but he must want nothing wrongly. He who loves wrongly, moreover, will never have all that he wants. The proper love must be identified, and it must be acted upon in due order.

Happiness—the good life—is to be found in a true appreciation of *caritas.* Still, even one who begins his quest for the good life with a great affection for his fellows may be ensnared. For, says Augustine, an apparent act of charity may in fact reflect the contempt of one who wishes to seem "greater because [he] didst bestow, than he upon who it was bestowed." [28] Pity and contempt go hand in hand and are too often the product of *superbia*—of pride. The spirit of *caritas* is thus contradicted in what only appears to be a manifestation of brotherly or neighborly love. Man's affections offer a beginning, but it is one that can be easily sidetracked.

That which drives people, Augustine observes, to any of the several objects of their love, is a personal sense of incompletion. *Desiderium,* that which Burnaby calls "the unsatisfied longing of the homesick heart," [29] is the key to understanding man's condition. The man of longings has but to fathom the depths of them in order to begin the true quest for his own good.

> This is our life, that by longing we should be exercised. But holy longing exercises us just so much as we prune off our longings from the love of the world. We have already said, "Empty out that which is to be filled." With good thou art to be filled: pour out the bad.[30]

Again, Augustine insists, look inside! Look inside to a longing for fulfillment—longing too often masked by baser needs.

Caritas—*The* Omnium Bonum

For Augustine, as we have noted, a good or *bonum* based on the acquisition of personal or material objects was incomplete. That is, a man who defines his existence in terms of external objects never discovers the real power of his own will. He is made to feel at best half a person, as he shapes his identity to the expectations of others. Because he never comes to know his inner self, he cannot properly love himself, nor can he willfully direct his own actions.

Action in service of the good of all was the goal of Augustine's writing and speaking. This action begins with the self, and is then extended to fraternal and social behavior. A new sort of mutuality becomes, after careful training, a genuine possibility. It is, he argues, much different to recognize a common commitment between two or more persons than for them to be dependent upon one another.

> If the *Summum Bonum* is by its very nature the *bonum commune,* a good which can be possessed only by being shared, then the desire and pursuit of it can never be desire and pursuit of a *bonum privatum.*[31]

Each gives himself to that which is common among them. A common ceding of power, Augustine insisted, is very different than dependence on other people. People can work together within a shared commitment to, and recognition of, a common good.

People would, he hoped, discover that this was the only way in which even a modicum of happiness could be reached. It was an approach that demanded more than a simple "desire to live happily." It insisted that people must as well *"will* to live *rightly"*[32] (emphasis added). To develop that will people must employ it in charitable action. The trinity within—memory, intelligence, and love—had regularly to be consulted.

> The trinity . . . was constituted this way: first we placed in the memory the object by which the perception of the percipient was formed; next, the confirmation, or as it were, the image which is impressed thereby; lastly, *love or will as that which combines the two*[33] (emphasis added).

The mobilization of love and will in the service of the common good thus entails the mobilization of both memory and intelligence. It permits free choice and action based on due deliberation of the past and present. It awakens "an holy longing" for that which lay beyond memory and tradition, habit and convention.

Temporal existence had significance for Augustine only insofar as people were made conscious of their ability to initiate change away from private feelings and material possessions. Once made conscious of that ability, they had to be stirred to a passionate commitment to such change, for "apatheia, passionlessness is not even our goal in the life to come. . . ."[34] A will compelled by want could, of course, lose its sense of direction. It could become the prisoner again of desires that led to dissatisfaction. Augustine, therefore, constantly had to demonstrate the glory of those objects of love that he espoused.

"Needy and unsatisfied, love is," he argues, "naturally subject to the things it loves. . . ."[35] The more excellent those objects, the more excellent the love and the more fulfilled the desire that accompanies it. "The happy life exists," he points out, "when that which is man's chief good is beloved and possessed." No one is happy, therefore, he continues, who does not enjoy what is man's chief good, nor is there anyone who enjoys this who is not happy.[36] The route to such happiness had been blocked by the slavish customs of imperial Rome. Augustine sought to open it for a will truly free to search for its own *bonum*. Only that will that was free could in turn act in accord with that *bonum*.

Caritas *as the Foundation of Authority and Community*

Caritas, is, as Anders Nygren suggests, a kind of synthesis between *Eros* and *Agape.*[37] Thus it combines Platonic training with Christ's example, and suggests as clearly as possible the parameters of the Augustinian-Christian community that we have been describing. That community is based on a combination of the strength and freedom of self-control and the authority and guidance of God's grace.

Augustine, the community builder, was faced with strategic problems. As a bishop, he clearly realized the practical absurdity of "the notion of universal appreciation of every human being by every other. . . ."[38] A universalistic perspective was important only if that perspective aided people in the immediate aspects of their daily lives. As bishop, he would attempt to create a context in which people could more easily develop genuine friendships. Through his monastery and in his congregations, he built centers within which friendships could more easily be initiated, sustained, and broadened into wider social patterns. Strong individuals involved in genuinely reciprocal relationships could form the basis, he hoped, of a renewed community.

Augustine sought to rebuild society from the bottom up. He knew well that "there was . . . no intrinsic good in extent of empire." On the contrary,

> large empire was like a rich man, "anxious with fears, wasted with troubles, burning with greed, never secure, always unquiet," always hoping for the quarrels of his enemies, while the small state was like the man of moderate means, "self-sufficient in his compact little patrimony," living modestly and contentedly with a secure conscience, "enjoying the sweetest peace with his kindred, neighbors and friends."[39]

No tinkering with imperial institutions would provide an adequate solution to these difficulties. Thus, Augustine even began to question any form of alliance between the church and the empire.

The corruptions of empire, moreover, emphasized the need for a more limited order. Love, Augustine insisted, was the source of that order. The more perfect the love that held a society together, the more ordered was that society. "The love of God for His creatures, the love of man for his God,"[40] these were the sustaining principles of both order and justice. Both of these were in turn derived from self-love and self-order. Far from being conservatizing or stagnant, his notion of order was in context radical and dynamic. The well-ordered individual or congregation had constantly to battle against the seductive alternatives of pagan culture. They strove to create a society that was very different from anything that most had seen during the entire period of the empire.

In the end, Augustine would offer a political therapy as a curative for late Roman ills. Like the more personal therapy of self-examination of his *Confessions,* his political therapy would reflect a sensitivity to the relationship between the developing individual and his human, social environment that was truly remarkable. The diagnosis and the cure are really very straightforward. Augustine was a sensitive psychologist who had to face social and political problems at the very instant that he was developing psychological and theological arguments.

Augustine's vision into his own life and times led him to search for what a contemporary ego psychologist has called a "margin of freedom"—one that might allow people to plan for a world in which Roman institutions would not offer the easy security that they had in the past. His mission was to prepare people to live in that world, to try to make them recognize the precarious nature of their existence, not to paralyze them with fear. Augustine hoped that people could become, as the same psychologist suggests, "more loving and relaxed and brighter in judgment. . . ." [41] Overcoming the debilitating aspects of personal failures, such people approach their lives with great energy and with a clearer sense of their goals. Augustine asked much the same of his fifth-century congregants.

The language of ego psychology may point to its own quasi-religious preoccupations as much as to Augustine's psychological sensitivity. The point is that these concerns are in the most fundamental of ways political, because they seek to create the foundations upon which people might engage in the common pursuit of shared goals.

Notes

1. *Epistle* 137.5.17, *A Select Library of the Nicene and Post Nicene Fathers,* vol. I, p. 480. *(Epistles.)*
2. *The City of God Against the Pagans,* 7 vols., The Loeb Classical Library, Harvard University Press, Cambridge, Mass., 1968–1972, XV, 16. *(DCD)*
3. Anders Nygren, *Agape and Eros,* Philip S. Watson, trans., Harper and Row, New York, 1969, p. 478. (Nygren)
4. *St. Augustine's Confessions,* 2 vols., The Loeb Classical Library, 1912, Book II, 60 *(Confs.)*
5. *Confs.,* III, 8.
6. John Burnaby, *Amor Dei,* Hadden and Staughton, London, 1938, p. 118. (Hereafter cited as Burnaby.)
7. *DCD,* XIX, 4.
8. "Ten Homilies on the Epistle of John, Homily VIII," 5, *Nicene and Post Nicene Fathers,* vol. VII, p. 508. (Hereafter cited "Ep. of John.")

9. "Sermons on Selected Lessons of the New Testament, Sermon XLVI," *Nicene and Post Nicene Fathers,* vol. VI, pp. 408–409.
10. *DDC,* I, 27.
11. Nygren, p. 541.
12. Cited in Burnaby, p. 121.
13. "Tractates On the Gospel According to St. John," XVII, 8, *Nicene and Post Nicene Fathers,* p. 114. (Hereafter cited as "On Gospel of St. John.")
14. *Confs.,* IV, 4.
15. Burnaby, p. 118.
16. *Confs.,* II, 6.
17. "Soliloquies," I, 23, *Nicene and Post Nicene Fathers,* Vol. VII, p. 545.
18. Ibid.
19. *De Libero Arbitrio,* I, 12, Migne, vol. 32. p. 1217. (Hereafter cited as *De Lib. Arb.)*
20. "On the Gospel of St. John," XVII, 8, p. 114.
21. The argument is strikingly parallel to that which Michael Walzer describes in speaking of Calvinism. See *Revolution of the Saints,* Harvard University Press, Cambridge, Mass., 1965, p. 56.
22. "On the Gospel of St. John," XVII, 8, p. 114.
23. Ibid., LXV, 1, p. 318.
24. Ibid.
25. *Epistle,* XCI, 1, p. 377.
26. Ibid., p. 378.
27. Burnaby, p. 168.
28. "Ep. of St. John," VIII, 5, p. 508.
29. Burnaby, p. 96.
30. "Ep. of St. John," p. 484.
31. Cited in Burnaby, p. 127. Again one is reminded of Rousseau's argument in the *Social Contract:* Freedom, he argues there, is that which "secures [men] from all personal dependence" (I, 7), and yet it is attained only by recognizing that which is shared by all. Each gives himself to that which is common. A common ceding of power, Augustine insisted also, is very different than dependence on other people. I'm dependent, you're dependent, and we will work together within that shared recognition. The message, thus becomes a utilitarian one—though it has been from the beginning for Augustine as well as Rousseau.
32. *De Lib. Arb.,* I, 14, p. 1237.
33. *De Trinitate,* XIV, 6.
34. Cited in Burnaby, p. 95.
35. Ibid., p. 165.
36. See, for example, Burnaby, pp. 49–51.
37. Nygren, chapter 2.
38. See, for example, *DCD,* XV, 16.
39. Cited in Ewart Lewis, *Medieval Political Ideas,* Alfred A. Knopf, New York, 1954, pp. 431–32. See also *DCD,* IV, 3, 15; V, 12, 17; XIX, 13, 21ff.
40. Sheldon Wolin, *Politics and Vision,* Little, Brown and Company, Boston, 1960, p. 123. The battle between order and disorder never ends. In its basic form, it was not unlike that described centuries later by Freud in *Civilization and Its Discontents.* Neither saw the possibility of overcoming certain tensions that are a necessary part of the very structure of life.

We shall never completely master nature; and our bodily organism, itself a part of nature, will always remain a transient structure with a limited capacity for adaptation and achievement. This recognition does not have a paralyzing effect. On the contrary, it points the direction for our activity. If we cannot remove all suffering, we can remove some, and we can mitigate some: the experience of many thousands of years has convinced us of that. As regards the social source of suffering [however], our attitude is different. We do not admit it at all; we cannot see why the regulations made by ourselves should not, on the contrary, be a protection and a benefit for every one of us. *(Civilization and Its Discontents,* W. W. Norton, New York, 1961, p. 73.)

Augustine faced the same dilemma. Civilization by its very nature, he argued, is hostile to the satisfaction of many individual desires, and so the individual may well face civilization with hostility. Augustine was fascinated by the process of accomodation thus necessitated. Like Freud, Augustine was interested in men's futile attempts to deal with these frustrations through the use of the many "substitutive satisfactions" offered by new and old tempters alike. He had attacked their use in Rome and, having diagnosed the disease, sought to cure it.

Augustine's therapeutic forum, was, of course, considerably different from Freud's. In some ways its group focus was far more limited and less intensive. In some ways the problems that he confronted were far more extensive and ambitious than Freud's, even the Freud of *Civilization and Its Discontents.* Augustine offered, as Freud did not, a political therapy. He sought to develop a more realistic view of society in order to encourage men to act to remove some of their sufferings and mitigate others. Augustine knew well the severity of the demands made by the commandments. His concern was to prepare men to respond to them while understanding that they could never be fulfilled. To overcome the temptations of which Freud and Augustine both wrote, men would have to be taught to face the nature of these temptations. There is more repression involved in the Augustinian message than any Freudian could be comfortable with, but there is also a search for solutions to social and political problems that push Augustine's psychology beyond Freud's and into a world of psychological insight that is a part of our own age.

41. Erik Erikson, "Identity and the Life Cycle," *Psychological Issues,* vol. I, no. 1, International Universities Press, New York, 1959, p. 75. Peter Brown's discussion of Augustine's notion of freedom suggests that for Augustine, "freedom cannot be reduced to a sense of choice: it is a freedom to act fully." *(Hippo,* p. 374.)

CHAPTER 5

Christian Language and Roman Politics: The Search for a Christian *Paideia*

> *For my part, I am nearly always dissatisfied with my discourse. For I am desirous of something better, which I often inwardly enjoy before I begin to unfold my thought in spoken words; but when I find that my powers of expression come short of my knowledge of the subject, I am sorely disappointed that my tongue has not been able to answer the demands of my mind. For I desire my hearer to understand; and I feel that I am not speaking in such a manner as to effect that.*
>
> De Catechizandis Rudibus, I, 6

George Orwell, writing of the English language in the twentieth century, suggests that,

> It is clear that the decline of a language must ultimately have political and economic causes: it is not due simply to the bad influence of this or that writer. But an effect can become a cause reinforcing the original cause and producing the same effect in an intensified form, and so on indefinitely.[1]

St. Augustine, writing about Roman rhetoric in the fourth century, confronted a similar dilemma. He recalled his own experiences as a student with horror. His instruction in rhetoric taught him to worry less about the subject of his oration than the style in which it was delivered. This emphasis had led him and his fellow students to neglect the proper use of language. Concerned less with the meaning of words than with the superficial effect that words had on others, they thought of words as playthings and of language as a game. The seemingly innocent games of the young were, he insisted, not to be ignored, because language games played between students and teachers inevitably would be played later by subjects and kings, citizens and governors.

Public Language and Public Virtue

Plato had warned that rhetoric could all too easily lose touch with virtue. Instead of providing a means to the attainment of the good, it often became an end in itself—an end that far from fulfilling worthy public goals actually confounded them. Augustine faced a comparable problem as he began to ask about his own education. Were words ends in themselves and rhetoric a sport concerned with nothing but "the conventional rules of letters and syllables?" [2] Augustine came to realize the hollowness of the skill in which he had been trained and in which he had begun to instruct others. Roman public words had lost any connection they might once have had with Roman public virtue.

Eventually Augustine would decide to withdraw his service from the "marketplace of loquacity" so that "young students should no longer buy at my mouth the weapons for their own madness." [3] Augustine's conversion had led him to recognize the dangers of treating words lightly. Even as he began his attack on Roman rhetoric, he initiated an effort to promote a new respect for language.

He saw language as a way of life, and he sought to create a new way of life through his new language. As David Burrell suggests, writing of Augustine's use of language, "the rules of inference which govern a particular language must become the rules of one's life, if he is to use that language with confidence and alacrity." [4] Augustine sought a new linguistic model, Burrell continues, one that at least would permit North Africans to recognize alternatives to Rome.

In the pursuit of this end he raised questions that were, in most cases, addressed in fundamentally new terms, and he offered some guidance in the creation of those terms for those to whom his writing and speaking was directed. The success of his enterprise—an effort to link ideas to action—was thus to a significant degree dependent upon (1) his own use of language, (2) his ability to promote a new arena for public debate, and (3) his facility in promoting new categories of analysis through which alternative policies might be formulated and debated.

Augustine, of course, understood that in the early stages of this enterprise people would have to be taught how to listen correctly. His

disillusionment with the superficiality of Roman rhetoric did not dam-
age his sensitivity to the spoken word. He would have appreciated full
well the significance of Max Weber's warning that a poor argument
could "turn a cause that is good in every sphere into a 'weak' cause,
through technically weak pleading." [5]

Indeed, Augustine saw in rhetoric a useful weapon and knew well of
the benefits of eloquence. He cautioned his reader not to be guilty of
the misuse of words characteristic of late Roman oratory, yet begged
for flexibility and encouraged colorful and expressive language. "We
must not," he insisted, "bridle our own language by restricting it to . . .
special meanings." [6] Rather, he urged, we must insure that it is easily
accessible to all. To be sure, he thought that religious language was
superior to philosophic language because it offered "a fixed rule in the
use of language," instead of the "verbal license" that could pervert
the truths of scripture.[7] Still, he opposed the view that the whole of the
scripture could be made clear by the use of interpretive rules. The rules
that he advocated were established to guarantee that the end of rhetoric—like the truths of religion—dominated mere technique. Insofar as
rhetoric and eloquence advanced the end of teaching, they were well
used.

The task of the Christian educator, despite his use of rhetoric, is thus
significantly different from that of his Roman, pagan counterpart. As
Ernest Fortin notes,

> The truth which the Christian is "persuaded" to accept is not a truth in
> any ordinary sense of the word but a beatifying or saving truth, which
> presupposes a decision on the part of the knower and which can be said
> to have been fully appropriated only when it issues in those deeds to
> which it points as its fulfillment. In and of itself it has the power to
> transform the individual who apprehends it. It is in one and the same act
> both theoretical and practical and thus transcends the dichotomy be-
> tween thought and action or between instruction and persuasion on
> which the classical understanding of rhetoric was predicated.[8]

Christian rhetoric, Augustine hoped, would bridge the gap between
private and public worlds, introducing into the world of politics an
important role for religious instruction and Christian belief. Since, for
example, "the ruler's power resides in his tongue," [9] Augustine stressed
the responsibility of a leader "to know what he ought to do and to do
what he knows." [10]

In their "childhood," the unity of the people of God had been sym-
bolized by a single language shared by all. The pride of those who
sought, naively, to build a "tower whose top will reach the heavens"

had been punished by God who "scattered them all over the face of the earth. . . ." Hence, "the name 'Confusion' was given to the city, because it was here that the Lord confused the speech of the whole world." Rulers who had in their pride "refused to understand God's commands so as to obey them [were] not [themselves] to be understood when [they] gave commands to men." [11] A significant dimension of the history of the people of God would from that time forward, Augustine suggests, entail a search for a common language through which a newly authorized leader might rediscover the possibility of the unity of the people of God and in turn act on that knowledge.

Of the many general and specific references to political leaders in the *City of God*, his discussions of David are the most telling for our purposes. David is praised for "the rational and proportionate symphony of diverse sounds" that he brought to his psalms. That harmony, Augustine suggests, "conveys the unity of a well ordered city, knit together by harmonious variety." David was a king as well as a writer of psalms, whose reign was to be praised as a combination of pious belief and ordered rule of "the young manhood of the people of God." As Augustine suggests in Book XVII of the *City of God*,

> Now David reigned in the earthly Jerusalem, being a son of the heavenly Jerusalem, greatly extolled by the divine testimony because his sins were overcome by such great piety." [12]

David's success as a ruler was surely in part a product of his use of language. His ability to communicate unity and harmony through his psalms at the very least symbolizes his abilities as a ruler. He had overcome his sins through piety and honed those skills through which he could convey to his people a sense of unity and harmony.

God had taken David "from the sheepfold" so that he might lead His people. With God's help, he had endured many hardships and defeated many opponents.[13] His integrity and dignity as an individual, developed through piety and humility, gave him that sense of confidence and wholeness needed to lead. The Israelites were in need of special instruction, if they were finally to be established as a people. David could speak to and instruct that people, precisely because that which he had endured personally paralleled that which God's people had endured collectively. He had now to communicate that sense of unity and wholeness that he had found as an individual to an entire people. In the following chapters, we will return to the history of this people and that period during which it emerges. For now, we must look at the general theory of language that informs and shapes Augustine's analysis of that history and lays the groundwork for his theory of leadership.

The Language of Christian Instruction—The Foundation of Public Order

Augustine wrote a great deal about language and its proper use in Christian instruction. As with the *Confessions,* we shall begin with his own advice, but here that advice is more explicit. Though there are many references to the function of words and the nature of language scattered throughout his works, there are three specific works with which we shall deal that address the problem of language as a central concern: *De Magistro, De Doctrina Christiana,* and *De Catechizandis Rudibus.* The first of these was a product of the years immediately after his conversion circa 387 A.D. The others belong to a more mature and public phase of his career. *De Doctrina* was begun in 396, but was not completed until 427 A.D. *De Catechizandis* was probably written in the midst of this effort circa 405 A.D.

Together, these three provide the basis for what Eugene Kevane has described as a Christian *paideia* or program of instruction. Augustine's insistence on the need for education has been clearly noted. The formal process through which this education is initiated has been clearly noted. Discussion of that process, has, however, been confined thus far to a discussion of his therapy of self-examination. Here we move beyond—though not away from—that therapy to the beginnings of a social and even political therapy. Augustine sought in these three works to establish the foundation of Christian culture and so of human civilization generally. After the fashion of the Greeks and Plato in particular, Augustine's *paideia* [14] was accompanied by a diagnosis of the human plight and a *therapeia* [15]—a provision for the remedy for that plight.

The most formal statement of his *paideia* and his *therapeia* appears in *De Doctrina Christiana.* Here he develops the notion of *doctrina* as the basis of Christian oratory and Christian instruction so as to criticize Rome and especially Cicero while introducing a Christianized Platonism. As Ernest Fortin again notes:

> The substance of that teaching is the "sound doctrine" of which St. Paul had spoken and in which the preacher has steeped himself through the assiduous reading and study of the Scriptures. Its cognitive status is therefore totally different from that of the pagan orator. Augustine's preacher teaches in a way in which even Cicero's perfect orator could never be said to teach. It is above all the superior dignity of that "teaching" which accounts for Augustine's inversion of the order of the rank of

the three functions performed by the orator. The duty to teach is not merely the Christian orator's first duty, it is his highest and in a sense his only duty.[16]

When framed by *De Magistro* and *De Catechizandis, De Doctrina* stands as the perfect complement to the *Confessions.* Written, for the most part, during the same years as his *Confessions, De Doctrina* introduces social or group remedies that Augustine combined with the therapy of self-examination of the *Confessions.* Augustine, like many other social critics,[17] knew that individualized remedies to problems caused by social and political disorders were destined to be partial at best. An individual, however nurturant his upbringing and healthy his individual circumstances, still had to become a part of a larger social and political whole. If he were to fulfill the promise of his particular situation, he would need social support. Lacking a broader community of support, he faced frustration and possibly even defeat of all that was so highly valued in his unique circumstances.

Augustine sought to build a linguistic and an instructional order that paid attention to individual and social, private and public, religious and political aspects of people's lives. The potential conflict within each pair was clearly recognized. His instructional task was to introduce the possibility that individual life could and should complement social life and private and public, religious and political life as well. Real conflict would remain, but true moral progress was possible only if knowledge of potential harmony were transmitted and acted upon. The transmission of that knowledge depended upon a renewed consciousness of the use of language by instructor and student alike. Then it might be possible to reevaluate the use of language in broader social and political contexts. Most importantly, Augustine insisted, it would not be possible either to convey such knowledge nor to act upon it without a renewed understanding of the way language functioned in both philosophic and moral discourse.

De Magistro

In his dialogue, *De Magistro,* Augustine took up the problems of teaching directly. It took the form of a discussion between Augustine and his son Adeodatus. Adeodatus, Augustine insisted, learned his most basic lesson early: "We speak," he said, "for the sake of teaching. . . ." Augustine reinforced that lesson.

> You as well as other men who judge matters suitably would reply to a garrulous word-lover who said: "I teach in order to talk" with "Man, why not rather speak in order to teach?" For if these things are true, as

you know they are, you truly see how much less words are to be es-
teemed than that for the sake of which we use words. For words exist in
order that they may be used, and in addition we use them in order to
teach. As teaching is superior to talking, in like degree speech is better
than words. So of course doctrine is far superior to words.[18]

It was not enough, however, simply to say that doctrine was superior.
It must be known why it was superior. Augustine confronted this issue
with a memory of the inadequacies of his own training. Rote learning
was not only insufficient but contrary to the example he hoped to illustrate—the example of Christ who "did not teach [men] words but
taught them things by means of words. . . ." [19] The kind of teaching he
had in mind was in part demonstrated by the very form of this discussion. The teacher questions the pupil and draws him out. To know that
doctrine was superior was not to have memorized a series of words or
formulae but to open one's mind to the possibility of a new kind of
truth—one not readily available in the Roman classroom. "For who,"
asked Augustine, "is so stupidly curious to send his son to school that
he may learn *what* the teacher thinks?" [20] The process should be one in
which the student learned *how* his teacher thought. Augustine wanted
much more for his son and other pupils than he had been given.

The problem facing the teacher was barely introduced here, but Augustine had developed an approach to a problem that he would pursue
for many years. Question the significance of words very carefully, he
implored. Beware, he cautioned Adeodatus, of those who are by "con-
sensus guardians of the rules of words." [21] A true understanding of
words and that which they signified was not to be found in their cata-
logues, for they were not interested in the truth of words. One can
never be certain, he insisted, that words "express the mind of a speaker
since a speaker may not know the things about which he speaks." [22]
The problem introduced is more complicated than that of the conscious
manipulation of words or deception. It is at the heart of the political
problem alluded to in the *Confessions*. The possibility of political
change was seriously limited by the lack of a language through which
men could discover that which they held in common.

Roman language reinforced the privatization that dominated that
culture in at least two ways. First of all, the diversity of languages
within the empire often meant that two people—regardless of their
good will—could not communicate with one another.

For their common nature is no help to friendliness when they are prevented by diversity of languages from conveying their sentiments to one
another; so that a man would more readily hold intercourse with his dog
than with a foreigner.[23]

But second and more disastrously, communication between two Romans was endangered by the competitiveness of Roman rhetorical custom such that,

> When a man seeking for the reputation of eloquence stands before a human judge while a thronging multitude surrounds him, inveighs against his enemy with the fiercest hatred, he takes no heed lest through the fury of his spirit he cut off a man from his fellow-men.[24]

Public language, such as it was, was formal and restricted. Rhetoric had become the tool of the "word lover," not the truth lover. The meaning of words had been replaced in importance by the superficial effect of words. "Good definers are hard to find," says Augustine, in part of course because they were not in demand. Augustine seeks to create that demand in this dialogue so that his son and his reader will not "attribute more to words than is proper," [25] but also in the hope that they will begin to use them as they were meant to be used—for a public purpose. Their very nature is public, he seems to argue, for they are meant to enable men to know one another, and to know that which they share with one another.

De Doctrina Christiana

The key to the solution of these basic problems of human communication, said Augustine in *De Doctrina,* lay hidden in the scriptures.[26] He sought in this work to discover a "way of discovering those things which are to be understood [of the scriptures], and a way of teaching what we have learned." [27] Both the discovery and teaching of scriptural doctrine required careful attention to the nature of signs.[28] Augustine's concerns here with conventional signs *(signa data)* or those signs through which men intentionally communicate with one another, as opposed to natural signs that without any intention make us aware of something beyond themselves—like smoke.[29]

There is in *De Doctrina,* then, an extension of arguments made in previous works. His discussion of signs was but the foundation of an examination of the human language and its roots in the human condition. Roman problems, he suggests here, merely exacerbated an already existing situation. His was a search for the cure of the disease that afflicted Rome rather than a mere treatment of the symptoms she manifested.

He worried, as suggested above, that words could become ends in themselves, diverting attention from meaning and emphasizing human weakness, flattery, and pride. The written word—the sign of a sign for

Augustine—was all the more susceptible to such distortion. Men, diverted by pride long before the Roman Empire, had become inured to the distortion and deception inherent in the nature of words as signs. To this the scriptures bear clear witness.

> These signs could not be common to all peoples because of the sin of human dissension which arises when one people seizes the leadership for itself. A sign of this pride is that tower erected in the heavens where impious men deserved that not only their minds but also their voices should be dissonant.[30]

The scriptures warn that the prideful use of a common language had led to dissension and the loss of that common language. This lesson, Augustine hoped, could help men to combat the source of that disension and regain that which they once had shared.

His search was for "the medicine of Wisdom." [31] Some of this medicine, he suggested would heal

> by contraries and others by similar things. He who tends the wounds of the body sometimes applies contraries, such as cold to hot, moist to dry, and so on; at other times he applies similar things like a round bandage for a round wound. . . .[32]

In the same way, Augustine sought the appropriate cures for the diseases of the psyche and the soul, the society and the polity. At times it seemed appropriate to point to the similarities between present and past discontents, as does the scripture in the Tower of Babel story, or as Augustine does in the *City of God* when speaking of the history of Rome. At other times, treatment seemed to call for the contrary example of the covenantal faith of the people of Abraham as an antidote to dissension. This use of words as treatment is the focus of his discussion of signs. One must understand the nature of words as signs but always with the proper end in view. That end is spiritual health—a wholeness, individual and social, much like that introduced in the *Confessions.*

As with the *Confessions*—which were being written at about the same time as these early sections of *De Doctrina*—there is a kind of dialectic at work. Men constantly face danger and despair in this life. The hope of faith is always balanced by an understanding [33] that there could be no perfect life on this earth. In *De Doctrina,* however, the movement between hope and despair is more direct. In fact, part of the process exemplified in his *Confessions* is here described. There are seven steps outlined in this work for the teacher to follow. The world in which he lived required that harsh measures be used to gain access to the reader.[34] He might in fact have to *frighten* an audience, thereby compelling it to listen. Such *fear,* combined with a deceptively easy *piety,* completed the first two steps in an almost rote mechanical fashion. Then, the pupil's attention gained, his piety could be nurtured and supplemented with *knowledge.* This knowledge would in turn offer the pious a new strength—*fortitude*—to confront the difficulties of his everyday life. Then and only then could he begin to see the nature of *mercy* and *love* in their proper light, for it took great courage to be merciful and loving in a world that did not highly value these virtues. Finally, lest he be fooled by his new mode of living, he had to be reminded of the inaccessibility of that final *wisdom* that was God's.[35] He dare not think that he was relieved of his responsibilities to face the continuing trials of this life with his brethren. Having learned of the possibility of public virtue and public action, he could not lapse back into the private luxury afforded by apathy.[36]

The formula appears to be very simple. Augustine knew that many had the talent to breathe hellfire and frighten their congregants into a shallow piety. This he hoped to avoid. The real test of the teacher was to deepen that piety. The third step—the development of knowledge—separated Augustine's sound doctrine from the dogmatic utterances of the kind that he had fought since he was a schoolboy. The process of discovery (so much more fully discussed in his *Confessions)* was now left behind, and the instructional mission of the work emerged. Augustine would spend the remainder of his argument looking for a "way of *teaching* what we have learned." [37]

The insight from which he began, both here and in his *Confessions,* was very basic. People would act together, for themselves, only when such action seemed feasible and the results predictable. Rome and Roman institutions provided a physical and a psychological block to such action. Augustine's strategy in confronting these blocks was to teach people of the limits of collective action, even as he told them of the possibility of such action. He hoped thereby to articulate an alternative to Rome that was accessible to the mind of his parishioner—one on which he could and would take action.

Augustine argued that no signs were "valid among men except by common consent." [38] He worried, however, about the source of people's agreement with one another.[39] Who taught them the rules of words? If it was the "guardians of the rules of words" [40]—those teachers of rhetoric who looked only for form—people had been trapped by Rome. These teachers were, Augustine insisted, the subtle tyrants of Roman culture. They fostered only passive cooperation, and encouraged the applause of the crowd. They ignored the fact that applause led neither to integrity for the speaker nor positive cooperation among the audience. Lacking these, there was no real communication between leader and led. All was reaction, anticipation.

Tempted to become the allies of demons, Romans did not recognize the opportunities for common action available to them. Augustine sought to teach them how to escape such a trap and so to fulfill their potential. Other teachers could, with the help of this work, begin to engage in activities in their own congregations and villages. They might begin to facilitate human interaction in support of the common good in pursuit of truth. Taking full cognizance of "those human institutions helpful to social intercourse in the necessary pursuits of life" [41] and combatting those that stood in the way of such intercourse, the teacher's words should have both a proximate and an ultimate end. [42]

De Catechizandis Rudibus

Augustine knew the importance of audience reaction. He worried in *De Doctrina* and in *De Magistro* about both the need to stir reaction through the proper use of words and the dangers implicit in so doing. When dealing with the uninstructed, these necessities and dangers were even more apparent.

Augustine composed *De Catechizandis Rudibus* in response to a deacon friend who wanted guidance in "the ministry of catechizing." In it he outlines in specific detail the kinds of questions that any teacher, but especially the teacher of the uninstructed, must consider.

The discussion is much less complicated here than that of *De Doctrina*, although the end served by each work was the same. In *De Catechizandis Rudibus*, Augustine addressed himself directly to the use of words in a statement that was also less theoretical and far more personal. The life and spirit of Augustine was embossed on each page as he tells his friend to "let the simple truth of the narration that we employ be like the gold which holds together in harmonious arrangement the jewels of an ornament without becoming unduly conspicuous." [43]

One may find that language is inadequate to express thought clearly, but that must not discourage the pastor.

> For my part, I am nearly always dissatisfied with my discourse. For I am desirous of something better, which I often inwardly enjoy before I begin to unfold my thought in spoken words; but when I find that my powers of expression come short of my knowledge of the subject, I am sorely disappointed that my tongue has not been able to answer the demands of my mind. For I desire my hearer to understand; and I feel that I am not speaking in such a manner as to effect that. [44]

Nonetheless, he insists, it is possible for the teacher to communicate his own enthusiasm and thus awaken interest in his audience, whether they are educated or uneducated, apathetic or alert. All of these can be approached if the teacher is aware of the nature and responsibilities of his task and takes personal delight in it. Indeed, he says, it is also important for the teacher to know the "articles of faith" of the scriptures and to know how to relate biblical stories, but these skills are not difficult to impart. The real challenge is to ensure that "the catechizer enjoys his work; for the more able to do so, the more agreeable will he prove." And so, of course, will anyone who would move people through his words to action.

Through all of this, the goal of "charity from a pure heart, and a good conscience and an unfeigned faith" [45] must be kept in view. People had to be moved away from self-satisfaction if they were truly to learn the lessons for which their attention had been elicited. They had then to be moved to discover for themselves a model that was different from that which Rome had offered.

Augustine worked to create a mode of public expression as an antidote to Rome. In *De Catechizandis Rudibus* he speaks, for example, of the power of sympathy:

> that when people are affected by us as we speak and we by them as they learn, we swell each in the other and thus both they, as it were, speak in us what they hear, while we after a fashion, learn in them what we teach.[46]

The reciprocity and mutuality involved here was, though different, no less serious than that which he hoped to capture in genuine friendships. Indeed, he offers an example that suggests the parallel. He asks:

> Is it not a common occurrence, that when we are showing to those who have never seen them before certain lovely expanses, whether of town or countryside, which we through often seeing already have been in the habit of passing by without any pleasure, our own delight is renewed at the novelty of the scene? And the more so, the closer the friendship between them and us. . . .[47]

So it is as well, he insists, for one initiated into the contemplative life. Here though, the friendship becomes more profound. Now rather than pause to admire the material,

> . . . . we wish to lift them up to the contemplation of the skill or design of the contriver, and hence have them soar upwards to the admiration and praise of the all-creating in whom is the most fruitful end of love.[48]

This passage, in some ways reminiscent of the discussion of love in Plato's *Symposium,* illustrates the kind of activity that could be prompted by words. This power to move men was clearly meant to affect more than their thoughts, and it was vital if Roman inertia was to be overcome.

Sermons to the People—Self-Discipline and Public Order

To attempt to summarize the sermons of a man who preached as often as five times a week for over forty years would be foolish and presumptuous. It is, however, possible to examine some of Augustine's sermons as a kind of test of his own suggestions. We can ask several questions, for example: How did he apply his own maxims? Is the sophisticated psychology found in more formal works like his *Confessions* also present in his sermons? Was he able to maintain rigorous attention to his substantive goals in the midst of sermons to people not as well trained as he was? Could he make himself a part of his congregation—personally and emotionally—and still keep them aware of God's purpose?

All these questions are crucial to the case being argued here, namely, that Augustine's attention to public questions and to the nature of the public thing (the *res publica)* has a political cast to it seldom recognized by political philosophers. A look at a selection of sermons that respond to these questions is by no means an attempt to generalize about all of them. It does suggest that the public and political concerns we have found in the *Confessions* and in his own arguments about the nature of language are elucidated in a most significant way in his sermons.

We have heard Augustine indicate in several places that eloquence could be dangerous.[49] Nonetheless, we would do well to remember with Sister M. Inviolata Barry "that the rhetor's art [Augustine] acquired in pagan schools had become second nature to the Bishop of Hippo."[50] They were talents moreover that made him a great success. As we have noted, whatever their danger, the skills of the rhetorician could be used for good as well as bad. One had first to learn the end toward which they were to be put, and then its use might become less threatening.

The Rhetoric of Self-Confrontation

Augustine knew well that he played a subtle and perhaps dangerous game in his use of rhetorical tricks. He sought to overcome these risks by directly confronting them. In fact, Augustine answers some of our questions in the text of his own sermons. His audience was clearly—

consciously and explicitly—a concern. He required that his audience be self-conscious of its responses to him. In one sermon, for example, his congregation responded to him and he asked: "My brethren, wherefore do you cry out, wherefore do you exult?" [51] He would not allow them to be carried off in an emotional response that could divert their attention or his. In yet another setting, he sensed problems in the response of his audience to a difficult scriptural passage and warned that,

> According to my ability . . . I have either explained to you or gone over with you a subject of great profundity. If any have failed fully to understand, let him retain his piety, and the truth will be revealed: and let not those who have understood vaunt themselves as swifter at the expense of the slower, lest in their vaunting they turn out of the track, and the slower more easily attain the goal. [52]

The truth of a lesson may be clarified by the skill of its instructor, but the truth must dominate, not the skill of the instructor nor the perspicacity of the pupil. However convenient Augustine's verbal facility, it was the spirit in which one approached difficult matters—one's inner motives and satisfactions—that were most vital to true understanding. The preacher must, he insisted, in his own sermon worry not only about his words and the difficulty inherent in communicating his ideas through them. He must also try to push his listener beyond a fascination with those words. His art must be one that weaves a captivating story with words, and yet leads his listener beyond them to his own freedom. This ability had been lost in Rome where the effect of the story became an end in itself. Thus, the success of the preacher was founded on his ability to instill a fascination with truth. The listener's role could not be passive, if the preacher was to attain his goal. He could not use Augustine's sermons to escape from the dilemmas of the fifth century. He had to confront them in the life of the sermon.

Augustine tells of this use of the sermon in a letter to his friend Alypius, Bishop of Thagaste at the time. [53] Concerned about the celebration planned for the anniversary of the birth of an early Bishop of Hippo, Augustine warned his congregation of the dangers of a custom that permitted drunken revelry on the occasion of the anniversary. Summoning up "all the power in thought and utterance which, in an emergency so great and hazardous, [God] was pleased to supply," he first awakened their attention by speaking of drunkenness. Then, seeing that resistance remained, he moved from one scriptural passage to another, attempting to move the recalcitrant first through fear and shame and then through tears of joy. Still, he reports, "so great was the power of detestable custom" that some remained unmoved. On the verge of quitting for want of "more powerful means," Augustine tells Alypius that he was visited by those whom he thought intransient and was moved to continue his preaching that finally met with success. The steadfastness of both preacher and congregant was thus shown to be of great importance. Augustine, employing a wide variety of styles and emotional appeals, succeeded in his attack on the power of custom and, moreover, in the end brought his congregation together in songs of praise, substituting a successful "spiritual feast" for the "carnal excesses in which others indulged." The former was made all the more sweet by dint of its contrast to the latter.

Whether confronting the lascivious conduct of his parishioners or interpreting the mysteries of scriptural allegory, Augustine sought constantly to challenge his audience. In fact, says van der Meer, "the sermons that most captured his hearers and called forth their delighted applause were just those that contained the most far-fetched allegories—the mystical antitheses and the correspondences of numbers." [54] These he often used to gain attention that was then quickly riveted on substantive goals. He had a way of dealing with the highest mysteries of faith while allowing "flashes of common wisdom to illuminate his pages" at the same time. The point of departure here is the same as that in his *Confessions*—his knowledge of himself. Barry suggests:

> His knowledge of himself gave him a great insight into human nature and his skill to present in a few words a person or a particular state of mind must have continually entertained his people.[55]

Self-knowledge gave him insight into what moved people—the people of his own congregation—to thought and action. Knowledge of language and rhetoric gave him insight into how such action could be evoked.

Christian Education and Inner-Worldly Asceticism

In his sermons, as in his writings, Augustine sought to build the self-discipline, endurance, and courage of his audience. He thus developed what Max Weber would later call "inner-worldly asceticism." As Weber suggests in talking of world religions:

> Active asceticism operates within the world; rationally active asceticism, in mastering the world, seeks to take what is creatural and wicked through work in a worldly "vocation" [inner-worldly asceticism]. Such ascenticism contrasts radically with mysticism, if the latter draws the full conclusion of fleeing from the world [contemplative flight from the world].[56]

Clearly, Augustine's "vocation" was no flight from the world. It was rather a rational and active confrontation with it. Though this life be filled with strife, Augustine argued, "we must endeavor and strain with all of our might that we may at last come to the most perfect peace." Commanded to live in concord and peace with one another, we must in the face of strife avoid the pitfalls of excessive hope on the one hand and despair on the other.

> . . . . Despair kills these; hope, those. The mind is tossed to and fro between hope and despair. Thou hast to fear lest hope slay thee; and, when thou hopest much from mercy, lest thou fall into judgment; again thou hast to fear lest despair slay thee, and when thou thinkest that the grievous sins which thou has committed cannot be forgiven thee. . . .[57]

This was a stern, harsh call to action, but one whose form was dictated by the nature of the world in which it was made, much as Calvin's would later be.[58] Augustine had every reason to believe that his mission would be resisted by many. His harshness was needed in the face of heretics who would shut out the church from all but the most pure, as much as it was needed to confront Roman culture.[59] His hope was to save Christianity for the common man in the face of the presumptuous attacks of both the well-educated pagan and the puristic heretic. It became necessary for him to strengthen the resolve of his parishioners against such attacks.

Thus, he again offers a lesson in applied psychology, or as Herbert Deane suggests, an understanding of the "psychology of fallen man." [60] He attempted to move men both to fear and to hope. The pessimism of Augustine was, as Deane notes, different from "the sense of despair and futility that marks so much of pagan philosophy in its later stages. . . ." [61] Sometimes with subtlety and indirection, sometimes explicitly with a heavy hand, Augustine would inveigh against the sins of lust and pride. Then, with astonishing regularity, he would tell his congregation why fear was necessary and even a prelude to hope:

> "The fear of the Lord is chaste, enduring forever." "The fear of the Lord"; not that distressing fear under the law, dreading exceedingly the withdrawal of temporal goods, by the love of which the soul commits fornication; but that chaste fear wherewith the Church, the more ardently she loves her Spouse, the more carefully does she take heed of offending Him, and therefore, "perfect love casteth" not "out" this "fear," but it endureth forever.[62]

He wanted men to fear the loss of God. God offered hope to the poor and strength to the failing. His mercy was undying. Still, none were perfect. Augustine pushed men between hope and despair with a constant understanding of what moved them to act. A new liberty may be found, he suggested, but one must never lose sight of the conflict that all must face.

> In part liberty, in part bondage: not yet entire, not yet pure, not yet full liberty. . . . For we have still infirmity in part, in part we have attained liberty. . . . From the fact that some infirmity remains, I venture to say that, in what measure we serve God, we are free; in what measure we serve the law of sin we are still in bondage.[63]

No one, including Augustine, escaped this bondage entirely. But men could work toward a liberty that might allow them to judge more freely that which they did in the face of conflict and temptation and also act together in militant struggle against temptation.

These were the words of a man interested in results. As Peter Brown suggests: "Augustine was certain of his basic role. It was not to stir up emotion: it was to distribute food." [64] Even his doctrine of predestination was tied to a theory of action.

> For Augustine's doctrine of predestination . . . was a doctrine for fighting men. . . . He had never written to deny freedom, merely to make it more effective in the harsh environment of a fallen world.[65]

Men were inevitably anxious beings, but their anxiety should not be wasted on things over which they had no control. There were, after all, things in the course of this world over which they and their wills had some control. As Brown suggests, Augustine never stopped trying to make these the primary focus of his teaching.

The unity of promise and performance (and of inner and outer man) that, for Augustine, had been forecast by the Greeks (and by the Old Testament people of Abraham) was destroyed by the formalized prating of the Roman orator spawned in a world devoid of genuinely public feeling. In an attempt to recreate that public feeling, Augustine prodded, implored, and exhorted his parishioners to a recognition of their active responsibilities toward themselves and their brethren. The *disciplina* [66] that he sought to create was one that could become the foundation of a new order with the congregation as the center of that order.

Augustine's political thought is as much involved with the creation of the unity and purpose of that congregation as it is with attacks on Roman institutions. His own definition of the people in the *City of God* is instructive: "A people," he says finally in Chapter XXIV of Book

XIX, "is the association of a multitude of rational beings united by a common agreement on the objects of their love." "It follows," he continues, "that to observe the character of a particular people we must examine the objects of its love." [67]

Augustine examined the nature of the people of Hippo and the objects of their love throughout his career, not solely in the *City of God*, but in early and more formal works and in his sermons to the people as well. His effort was clearly to help clarify and redefine those objects—to direct them to a confession of love of God and so to a new public regard. Insofar as this is accomplished, the Christian congregation became the source of a new definition of the people of Hippo. His goal thus became a political goal in the terms of his own argument about the nature of politics, for it was the object of their love that gave substance and direction to the political order.

Notes

1. George Orwell, "Politics and the English Language," in *The Collected Essays, Journalism and Letters of George Orwell*, Harcourt, Brace and World, New York, 1908, p. 127.
2. *St. Augustine's Confessions*, 2 vols., The Loeb Classical Library, 1912, I, 18. (*Confs.*)
3. *Confs.*, IX, 2.
4. David Burrell, "Reading the Confessions, An Exercise in Theological Understanding," *Journal of Religion*, vol. 50, 1970, pp. 338–40.
5. Max Weber, "Politics as a Vocation," in Hans Gerth and C. Wright Mills, eds., *From Max Weber: Essays in Sociology*, Oxford University Press, New York, 1958.
6. *The City of God Against the Pagans*, 7 vols., The Loeb Classical Library, Harvard University Press, Cambridge, Massachusetts, 1968–1972. XIV, 8. (*DCD*)
7. Ibid., X, 23.
8. Ernest Fortin, "Augustine and the Problem of Christian Rhetoric," *Augustinian Studies*, vol. 5, 1974, p. 93. (Fortin)
9. *DCD*, XVI, 4.
10. Cited in Fortin, p. 94.
11. *DCD*, XVI, 4.
12. Ibid., XVII, 20.
13. Ibid., XVII, 8.
14. Eugene Kevane, "Augustine's Christian Paideia," in *Augustinian Studies*, Annual Publication of the Augustinian Institute, Villanova University, vol. 1, 1970.
15. See Robert E. Cushman, *Therapeia: Plato's Conception of Philosophy*, University of North Carolina Press, Chapel Hill, 1958.
16. Fortin, p. 92.
17. Augustine's argument is not unlike that of Plato before and many after, including as different social and political commentators as Jean Jacques

Rousseau, Erik Erikson, and Robert Coles. For each, the individual—Augustine's Christian *catechumen,* Rousseau's Emil, Erikson's young American, Coles' young migrant—requires a broader and healthy social context in which to grow as an individual.

18. *De Magistro,* Migne, vol. 32, p. 1210. (Hereafter cited as *DM.)*
19. Ibid., p. 1195.
20. Ibid., p. 1220.
21. Ibid., p. 1204.
22. Ibid., p. 1218.
23. *DCD,* XIX, 7.
24. *Confs.,* I, 18.
25. Ibid., p. 1220.
26. *De Doctrina Christiana,* Migne, vol. 34, "Prologus," pp. 15–19. (hereafter cited as *DDC)*
27. Ibid., p. 19.
28. *DDC,* 1–2. In *De Doctrina,* Augustine defined a sign in the following way:

    A sign is a thing which causes us to think of something beyond the impression the thing itself makes upon the senses (II.1.1).

    The notion of causality in the definition is suggestive of Augustine's concern with linguistic theory as a pastoral tool. This was made even more clear as he distinguished between natural and conventional signs in *De Doctrina.*

    Those are natural *(naturalia)* which without any desire or intention of signifying make us aware of something beyond themselves, like smoke signifies fire. . . . Conventional [data] signs are those which living creatures show to one another for the purpose of conveying, in so far as they are able the motion of their spirits or something which they have sensed or understood. Nor is there any other reason for signifying, or for giving signs, except for bringing forth and transferring to another mind the action of the mind in the person who makes the sign (II.1.2).

    His enterprise was clearly stated. He sought to examine and better understand human communication—human communication that is intentional!

29. Ibid., II.1.1.
30. *DDC.,* II, 4.
31. Ibid., I, 14.
32. Ibid., I, 18.
34. Peter Brown makes this argument in his biography, as does van der Meer in his study, *Augustine the Bishop.*
35. *DDC,* II, 7.
36. The pattern here is much like that of the *Confessions* with the triad of fear, hope, and anxiety now elaborated in seven steps. He was writing the two works at roughly the same time, so that the parallel is a natural one. In some ways, then, this can be seen as an elaboration of what we have called the "dialectic of guilt and praise."
37. *DDC,* "Prologus."
38. Ibid., II, 25.
39. Again Markus' objections are interesting, but not in keeping with the focus

of this study. In some ways it makes more sense to view Augustine's comments here in the same way that one would view discussions of the emergence from the state of nature in Rousseau or Hobbes.

40. *De Magistro,* Chapter 5, Migne, vol. 32, p. 1202.
41. *DDC,* II, 39.
42. The older Augustine reflected in the later chapter of *De Doctrina* is clearly less optimistic about the use of human institutions; but his purpose as a teacher retains an interest in the immediate, public lives of his parishioners. For example, in Book III, Chapters XII–XIV, he engages the reader in a series of discussions of charity, but in the context of local customs and habits, insisting on the need for the flexibility of the pastor according to the circumstances of his parish.
43. *De Catechizandis Rudibus,* I.6, Migne, vol. 40, p. 317. (Hereafter cited as *DCR.)*
44. Ibid., I, 2, p. 311.
45. Ibid., I, 3, p. 313.
46. *DCR,* I, 12, p. 323. Augustine is fully aware that different men will require different kinds of instruction. He is, for example, particularly concerned with the problems posed by one who is trained in the arts of rhetoric. While he has some advantage, argues Augustine, he knows well from his own youth that he also has more to overcome than the less-skilled but less-corrupted student.
47. Ibid.
48. Ibid.
49. In fact, we have heard him criticize the servile respect that some of his contemporaries manifested. See *On Christian Doctrine,* Library of Liberal Arts, The Bobbs-Merrill Co., Inc., New York, 1958, "Introduction," p. xvii.
50. Sister Inviolata Barry, "St. Augustine, the Orator," *Patristic Studies,* Catholic University of America, Washington D.C., vol. VI., p. 253. Sister Inviolata's study is detailed and complete. She outlines and describes the manner in which Augustine imitates and develops a wide variety of classical rhetorical devices. Her work is of great help to anyone who would begin to understand the complexities of Augustine's sermons to the people. Our task, is, however, considerably removed from hers. Beginning with her documentation, we shall investigate the ways in which Augustine blended his understanding of history, rhetoric, and Christian doctrine.
51. St. Augustine, "Homilies on the Gospel of John," *The Nicene and Post Nicene Fathers,* vol. VII, p. 25.
52. Ibid., p. 254b.
53. Ep. XXIX, *The Nicene and Post Nicene Fathers,* vol. 1, p. 253ff.
54. F. van deer Meer, p. 447.
55. Barry, p. 258.
56. Max Weber, "Religious Rejections of the World and Their Directions," in Gerth and Mills, p. 325.
57. "On the Gospel of John," *The Nicene and Post Nicene Fathers,* vol. VII, p. 199b.
58. Peter Brown, *Augustine of Hippo,* p. 390. See as well, Deane, and Calvin, *On God and Political Duty.*
59. Ibid., p. 221, 229. Brown suggests that "Augustine showed himself a stern victor. In a sermon preached to a simple audience, he dismissed the Pel-

agians and Caelestians: these "wind bags," puffed up with pride, had dared, in the face of the thunderous words of the Apostle, to deny "that nobody in this flesh, nobody in this corruptible body, nobody on the face of this earth, in this malevolent existence, in this life full of temptation— nobody can live without sin. Let them and their cleanliness be outside" (p. 363). Stern, yes, but in the face of a call for purity that could potentially at least, be far more threatening to this "simple People."

60. Deane, chapter II.
61. Ibid., p. 66.
62. *En. en Ps.,* p. 161.
63. "On the Gospel of John," p. 233b.
64. Peter Brown, *Augustine of Hippo,* p. 252.
65. Ibid., pp. 403–404.
66. Ibid., chapter 21.
67. *DCD,* Loeb, XIX, 24.

CHAPTER 6

Auctoritas and *Libertas:*
An Introduction to Augustine's
Theory of Leadership

Our very mind, that natural seat of reason and understanding, is enfeebled by certain old faults that obscure its clarity and is prevented not only from embracing and enjoying, but even from enduring the unchangeable light until this mind has been renewed from day to day and so healed, thereby becoming equal to such felicity, it had first to be dipped and soaked in faith and so cleansed.

DCD, XI. 2

Augustine's concerns with the problems of freedom and authority led eventually to a discussion of the nature of leadership and, in the *City of God,* to a specific discussion of political leadership. His task remained one of building community from the bottom up, but his psychological and political sophistication led him to the recognition that it was necessary to be concerned with the whole context in which that community develops. The church—offering as it did a place within which individuals could reexamine themselves and their relationships with others—provided only part of the answer. Other social and political institutions had to be encouraged to foster renewal as well. It was clear to Augustine that Roman political and social institutions and Roman leaders had, by and large, failed to offer such guidance and encouragement. The *City of God* was his attempt to illustrate that failing and to offer an alternative to Rome and her style of leadership.

119

Looking to Rome, to the people of Abraham, and to the people of the Christian era, Augustine examined three modes of leadership within each era and cultural milieu. He looked first to the origin of each people—the Roman, the Abrahamic, and the Christian, and he argued that the founder's activities were critical to the ongoing nature of each of these societies. Secondly, he recognized the problems that confront the "stabilizing leader"—the problems of maintaining peace and stability in an already existing polity that is presumably functioning smoothly. He again compared various leadership styles between the three cultures in question, and concluded that the stabilizing leader faces grave difficulty when confronted with any sort of crisis or disruption, unless he is able to evoke a sense of that common interest and shared dedication instilled in that people at the time of its origin.

This last problem led him to consider a third leadership role that he also found in these three traditions—a role that is closest to his own. It may be necessary, he suggested, for an intermediary to appear who is charged with reminding both the people and its leaders of the nature of their origins and their corresponding commitments to one another. The everyday problems of state can deflect the leader's attention from such fundamental problems. The natural concerns of private individuals for their own welfare and security may push such issues into the background. The political educator *(magister)* consequently is needed to prepare for and compel a confrontation with crisis.

Augustine thus never moved far from the basically instructive or edifying mode that characterized his *Confessions*. The *City of God* suggests the broad scope of that mode, as he asked that his reader examine the memory of a people to find therein some clues about the identity of that people. His audience was an increasingly large group of well-educated Romans. His task was to defend his community and to provide for its sustenance. He offered a most fundamental critique of the nature of Roman society from its origins, and then presented an alternative—a new remembrance—that might be seen as both the predecessor of and a model for the Christian era—the Abrahamic tradition. His role remained fundamentally pastoral, but it took on new dimensions through the *City of God*. The theme of self-examination introduced in his *Confessions* expanded to include the history of social and political organization.

The Search for Authority

Augustine's concern with the nature of leadership was shared by many in the later Roman Empire. As one commentator suggests, "people felt they needed protectors" and sought them in many places, "in Heaven as well as on earth." [1] Augustine knew that this search was crucial, but he knew as well that men could easily be deceived. He wrote with a "deep sense of insecurity, a fear that civilization was something balanced precariously on the edge of a volcano from which anarchy might burst forth at any time." [2] Such an atmosphere of crisis demanded leadership, but did not offer men the luxury of balanced and careful judgment. On the contrary, the same sense of urgency that moved Augustine to search for an alternative to a decaying Roman culture provided a backdrop for those who would promote insecurity as the necessary foundation for their power.

Augustine also knew, from personal experience, the lure of inaction and submission. The harsh insecurities of the time undermined confidence and the will to act, while creating a desperate eagerness to accept any comforting answer. Later Roman men were, he felt, "enfeebled by certain old faults that obscure" the clarity of reason.[3] He began, as did his enemies, by making use of such weakness, but his aim was not to freeze men in their anxiety. Rather, he hoped to prompt them to a recognition of it and hence to a new activism. As he suggested in the *City of God:* "For in this region of weakness and in these evil days such anxiety is also not without its uses in causing [people] to see with a keener longing that place of safety where peace is most complete." [4]

Once again, then, Augustine assumes the role of therapist. Now, however, he looked beyond individuals to the social and political groups that they comprise, beyond parents and teachers to kings and magistrates, priests and bishops.

Men could be deceived in a radically insecure world, but Augustine insisted that they could also be led to new and greater heights.[5] However, any leader who attempted to attain those heights would be forced to accept extraordinary burdens. It would not be enough to win followers for himself, persuading them to accept some alternative model of life and society. Human beings were too ready to follow any plausible and eloquent orator who played on their weakness and desperation. (That observation, obviously, is evident in his critique of Roman rhetoric.) The *magister*—the statesman of an age of crisis—must find or create in his public the strength and independence necessary to judge the substantive merits of his own case. The foundation of Augustine's theory and practice of leadership is thus twofold: he must make his appeal in a form that will capture the attention of his audience, but he must also educate that audience, giving it the knowledge and character to distinguish and reject would-be statesmen and unworthy teachings.

There is little doubt that men did seek alternative forms of social existence. The proliferation of sects and monasteries surely speaks to this. As one commentator suggests, these were "new creations of new men" and an indication that many had come to "act out their inner life through suddenly coagulating into new groups." [6] Many men, including the young Augustine, had been too easily seduced by them. Thinking that they were "new men" and that their creations were "new worlds," they were, Augustine argued, in fact victims of the Roman culture in which they grew and to which they responded. His concern for Everyman—the ordinary North African—led him to search for alternatives that were at once broader and more penetrating than those offered by monks and sectarians. Augustine hoped that a broad spectrum of men could be made to realize both the necessity and significance of a social rebirth. Certainly, many men (organized and unorganized) needed to develop critical faculties through which alternatives were to be assessed.

Augustine had no doubt that men would seek guidance. Augustine would have agreed with a contemporary observer who suggests that though "men are said to hate authority . . . experience belies it. It is true that intimidatory imperatives arouse resentment in them, but it is no less true that they are ever seeking imperatives to guide them." [7] There was no lack of imperatives in the late Roman world, but how were men to make reasonable assessments of their worth? For Augustine, the individual was the foundation of social rebirth. He will seek an authority that can give unity and sense to his life, but he must be taught that not just any authority will do.

The Roman Empire

The *City of God* is an attempt to use Rome and Roman institutions as vehicles for a public instruction, which was intended to awaken men to their enslaved existence. As G. H. Allard suggests:

> In this light [viz. the theory that Augustine's pastoral duties are crucial to his writing of the *City of God* as they were to many of his works], Augustine's intention appears more clearly. In fact the literary genre of a work is always related to the author's intention and one can usually comprehend the one in the other. Cast in the scheme of the catechetic genre, the *City of God* follows a profound purpose, that of a catechism of happiness to which Augustine was personally sensitized and to which peoples' minds were receptive given the fall of Rome and the fragile eternity of the Empire.[8]

The *genre catechetique* found a new and much broader audience, as Augustine addressed himself to the people leaving Rome after 410 A.D.

Augustine's attack on pagan institutions was now more direct. Political decay had become more real. Public questions were more pressing. The history of Rome became, in Augustine's hands, a study of human nature that he hoped would alert the attentive and self-conscious reader, offering him a political therapy to supplement the "therapy of self-examination" of his *Confessions.*

Augustine found Rome's attention to questions of social unity and public virtue admirable but seriously incomplete. In fact, Roman society was paralyzed by a blindness to its past and obeissance to opinion. His critique began with the most obvious, and proceeded to examine the underlying causes of what he describes as public atrocities.[9] The corruption of public morals had been reinforced through an unwarranted celebration of the past. Only through looking first at the deception and the pain of the past could a people confront its present discontents and so recognize otherwise masked deficiencies in the Roman state. Even a "most learned and weighty celebrity" like Varro had been taken in by prevailing custom, and so proved unable to examine thoroughly the nature and direction of Roman society.

Varro's problem, on the other hand, is that he was "afraid to oppose the beliefs and customs of the people, altogether vicious as they are (and as he knew them to be), where superstition appears in public rites." Thus trapped by "public dogma," his analysis of "public virtue" was severely limited.[10] Belief had come to be defined by prevailing opinion. Opinion was in turn ruled by superstition and hollow custom. Though Varro knew custom to be antagonistic to true public virtue, his inability to confront either custom or opinion left him without an audience for his instruction, and thus made his instruction suspect.

Augustine never doubted that belief was necessary to society. He worried only that belief was more complex than many in his day had come to assume. Philosophers and ordinary men were alike in their lack of understanding. Gods of all sorts, even those who represented the clearest violation of civic virtue, were regularly defended by Varro. The result in Augustine's words was that men were "bound together in a friendly society of deceivers!" [11] He sought belief that might lead to trust, belief that could offer men the foundation for a shared existence. Without it, he worried, men would be too easily distracted by appearance and show. Uncritical belief might lend men a temporary unity, but not one that could withstand a period of crisis. As long as men remained uncritical and unselfconscious, their desire to be entertained would blind them to the difficulties inherent in a truly public existence.

The gods that Varro called upon to reinforce the bonds of civil association, Augustine saw as akin to those produced by the poets' myths. Men liked to be entertained and this was the job of poets who invented their gods, who "write to please not to benefit." [12] What Varro had failed to comprehend was that his civil theology was constructed to appeal to the same need for entertainment.

> If the poets were to invent tales like this and the mimes to act them out, they would undoubtedly be assigned to the mythical theology and thus banished from the high estate of the civil theology. But our great scholar publishes these scandals, not as poetic inventions, but as *public dogma;* not as a part of the mimes, but as a part of the sacred rites; not as belonging to the theaters, but to the temples—in short not to the mythical, but to the civil theology [13] (emphasis added).

Augustine took great pains in the *City of God* and elsewhere to reaffirm the significance of tradition and religious custom.[14] His argument here is that Varro and others had deceived themselves. In fact, Roman gods, he argued, played only a secondary role in binding men's lives together into a peaceful civil association. Religion and belief, rather than providing the cement of society, had become diversions—propaganda that turned the attention of men away from the real source of their unity. The unity of Rome was in reality the result of conquest, and was maintained in an atmosphere of crisis and deception. The social harmony for which Augustine sought was one that had to grow internally and produce public belief. Roman peace was imposed externally and maintained by public dogma.

The strength of the whole was dependent on the strength of its parts. Roman statesmen and philosophers had lost sight of this simple maxim and were, therefore, trapped into supporting a self-contradictory system based on a conflict between private needs and external force. The more men sought to further private aims, the more force would be required to maintain peace. A peace based on deception or force, Augustine felt, would be increasingly difficult to maintain. Varro and others had failed to recognize that the peaceful and the good order are identical, and that a good order depends on good men.

So, the good leader must seek to educate his people so that they will recognize pleas made on their behalf. A rule based on force, said Augustine, is inherently weak, because it eschews education and so has a weak base of support. Individuals do not look to such a rule as the author of civil harmony—one to respect and from which to seek counsel. Instead, they seek to hide from it, to protect their individual interests as best they can, or to curry favor with a demeaning flattery. Insofar as Rome's unity had become dependent on such feeling, it had become fundamentally weakened. The logic of Roman rule was premised on fear and insecurity. Consequently, fearful and insecure men were implicitly the good citizens of Roman political practice. The praxis of Roman politics was the antithesis of the classical political ideal.

Augustine's attack on Rome was thus an attack not so much on political leadership as an attack on antileadership. Roman statesmen, philosophers, and citizens had all lost sight of the fundamental requisites of such leadership.[15] Romans spoke of public virtue as though it were a given, thereby failing to confront the most serious challenge to philosopher and statesman alike. Virtue, says Augustine, "is not among the primary things of nature," but is "ushered in by instruction." [16]

What is missed by the Roman philosophers, he continues, is the challenge of that instructional task. Instead of comprising a list of virtues, it was necessary to address the minds of men who were continually tempted by the opposite of virtue. The activity of virtue in this life is a "perpetual war with vices, not external vices, but internal, not alien, but clearly our very own. . . ." [17] None of the four cardinal virtues—temperance, prudence, justice, and fortitude—is found unchallenged in this life.

> Far be it from us, then, so long as we are engaged in this internal war to hold it true that we have already attained to that happiness which is the goal that we would gain by victory. And who is so wise that he had no battle at all to wage against his lusts? [18]

The real problem, said Augustine, is the problem of leading that battle, lest even partial victory be hindered.

Augustine's Alternative

Augustine celebrated life and the virtues that promoted the good life.[19] He felt that Roman virtue, as taught, failed to do either. Unlike the Roman philosophers, Augustine did not impute to these virtues "such powers as to say that men in whom they reside will suffer no misery." [20] The unreality of such a claim was bound to end in the frustration of any who believed it. Augustine instructed his readers in "true piety," which could lend reality to classical virtues and allow men to "look forward with endurance" to true happiness.[21] Christian piety taught people to understand their limitations, and so gave them a more realistic sense of what they could accomplish.

Endurance is alert and dynamic, not static. Augustine looked for men, or those qualities in men, that confront the difficulties of life actively—appreciating their limits but also affirming that which they can accomplish. As he had done in his *Confessions,* Augustine placed the trials of human existence in a universal perspective, not to belittle them, but to give men a clearer sense of what could be done in this life. He agreed with philosophers who argued that

> a man should be brought into harmony with himself and therefore instinctively avoid death, and *that he be his own friend* in such wise as to be vigorously determined and eager to keep the breath of his life and to live on in his union of body and soul [22] (emphasis added).

If men were to live such lives, however, they would need much assistance—the direction and guidance of teachers and leaders and the support and fellowship of good friends. Insofar as Rome had failed to offer such direction, to guide men in their battles between virtue and vice, its moralizing was empty. Unable "to be his own friend," the Roman about whom Augustine worried was unable to find friends among his fellows. In a time of relative calm, such isolation could be bearable. Rhetoric about public virtue could replace its reality. Disturbed about this state of affairs generally, Augustine worried that men would find themselves either immobilized in the face of crisis or driven to fanaticism. He had clear evidence that both options were exercised. He offered a third choice—one that might renew not just the rhetoric of public virtues but renew the men, whose understanding of those virtues was required to give substance to what he feared had become mere form.

Religion, he insisted, had an important role to play in this world. Its ultimate end may be in the next world, but Augustine attacked those—pagan and Christian alike—who argued that religion has value only in the life to come.[23] He attacked the pagan gods for failing to deal with the "life and morals of the cities and nations that worshipped them." [24] He quotes Persius' *Satires* and asks where such standards are enforced.

> Come and learn, O miserable souls, and be instructed in the causes of things: learn what we are, and for what sort of lives we are born; what place was assigned to us at the start; how to round the turning post gently, and from what point to begin the turn; what limit should be placed on wealth; what prayers may rightfully be offered; what good there is in fresh minted coin; how much should be spent on country and on kin; what part God has ordered you to play, and at what point of the human commonwealth you have been stationed.[25]

The church with less lofty claims has addressed itself to the problem of the human commonwealth far more effectively than has Rome. The problem, as he noted in his *Confessions,* is the method of philosophers. They were unable to show men the way to happiness. They knew only how to talk about it.

How much more satisfactory as a means to train the young in virtue if there were public recitations of the laws of the gods instead of vain praise of the laws and customs of our forefathers! For all the worshippers of such gods, when once they have been driven by lust "imbued" as Persius says, "with burning poison," would rather contemplate deeds of Jupiter than the teachings of Plato or the opinions of Cato.[26]

Augustine's task was to find a way to make such teachings accessible to the people he addressed. Men would first have to be made aware of the difficulties of this life and then taught to pass beyond them so alternatives could be judged fairly. The distractions were so powerful that, unless they were first exposed and surmounted, men would never, he felt, get beyond them. Men could gain the necessary perspective only through comparison with a more perfect order, but that order would have to be taken seriously.

That which men need, he says, is accessible to them. God speaks to man, but to that in man which is superior to all of the rest of his substance, that which opens men to the possibility of a new way. The problem is that:

Our very mind, that natural seat of reason and understanding, is enfeebled by *certain old faults* that obscure its clarity and is prevented not only from embracing and enjoying, but even from enduring the unchangeable light until this *mind* has been *renewed* from day to day and so healed, thereby becoming equal to such felicity, it had first to be dipped and soaked in faith and so cleansed [27] (emphasis added).

Clearly, men were educable. They could be taught to be more independent than they were—to be more able judges of the events that controlled their lives. They were often, but not always, deceived, and they could be educated towards a better life. Augustine sought to develop a mind that could "endure instead of fleeing from a distressful life, and that [could] in the light of pure conscience despise the judgment of men, especially that of the mob, which as a rule [was] wrapped in a fog of error." [28] The strong mind, he said, "is one that exhibits self-respect guarding against dishonour." [29] People could not, however, find such strength simply by looking within themselves, for their "natural seat of reason" had been enfeebled. They had to be directed by a new kind of authority that they could respect—not one to which they had to yield, but one that could lead men to a new understanding of their limitations. Only then, argued Augustine, could men truly recognize their potential.

Yves Simon's argument approximates Augustine's:

> Thus the proposition that authority is necessary to the intention of the common good has a double meaning. It means, first, that authority is necessary in order for private persons to be directed toward the common good; it means, second, that authority is necessary in order for functional processes, each of which regards some aspect of the common good, to be directed toward the whole of the common good.[30]

Man is thus given some preliminary direction within which he can act. Without such direction, freedom is suspect or at least less full. As Simon suggests:

> Nothing is further removed from freedom than the indetermination of matter, for freedom is mastery and proceeds not from a lack of determination but from a particularly full and hard kind of determination.[31]

Augustine would have agreed. His notion of *libertas* was not, as M.J. Wilks has noted, "freedom from authority and law." [32] On the contrary, he saw freedom and authority as partners. What good is freedom of choice, if men lack the capability to judge between alternatives?

His aim, therefore, in the *City of God,* as it had been in his *Confessions* and other earlier writings, was to discover a new authority. As was the case in the early writings, the scriptures are central to this authority. Likewise, Augustine himself becomes a respected authority. The introducer and interpretor of the scriptures, he points the way and makes them accessible to Everyman. In addition, in the *City of God* Augustine introduces history—specifically the histories of entire peoples—to discover the source of the legitimacy of the authorities respected by those peoples. In so doing, he becomes a civic or political therapist as well as an individual therapist. He defines and seeks to influence those objects that a people share and love in common. He describes thereby the most basic substance of a commonwealth, and he offers instruction in the reformation of that basic substance.

Notes

1. Peter Brown, *Religion and Society in the Age of Augustine,* Harper and Row, New York, 1972, p. 68. (Hereafter cited as *Religion and Society.)*
2. Michael J. Wilks, "Augustine and the General Will," *Studia Patristica,* vol. IX, pp. 488–520.
3. *DCD,* XI, 2.
4. Ibid., XIX, 10. Authoritarian personality arguments may grow out of such comments. It is argued here that Augustine is attempting to combat just such tendencies, and believes that he has begun to do so.
5. See note number 82 in the preceding chapter.
6. Peter Brown, *Religion and Society,* p. 13.

7. Bertrand de Jouvenel, *Sovereignty,* Phoenix Books, University of Chicago Press, Chicago, 1957, p. 75.
8. G.H. Allard, "Une Nouvelle Interpretation de la Civitas Dei," *Studia Patristica,* vol. IX, 1963, p. 339.
9. *DCD,* IV, 1. He summarized his attack on certain public spectacles in the fourth book of the *City of God:*

> It was also my duty to show that the false gods whom they once worshipped openly and still worship secretly are unclean spirits, and most malign deceitful demons, so much so that they find amusement in crimes which whether real or fictitious, are in any case their own, for they have chosen to see them solemnly presented in their honour during their public festivals. The result is that human weakness cannot be restrained from perpetrating damnable deeds, as long as supposedly divine authority is given to the imitating of these deeds.

> All this was not the fruit of my own conjecture; I cited evidence, some of it that of recent events that I recall, for I myself have seen such spectacles presented in honour of such deities, and some of it that of the writings of men who left to posterity descriptions of these things, not as a reproach, but for the honour of their gods. Take Varro, for example, who in the eyes of the pagans is a most learned man and a most weighty authority. When he wrote a treatise in two parts, one on the human and one on divine things, he alloted some books to human things, and the others to divine, and assigned each topic to the level that he deemed proper to it. He gave theatrical shows a place not at most among human, but among divine things, although certainly if there had been none but good and respectable men in the state, the theatrical shows could have had no place even among human things.

10. Ibid., VI, 6.
11. Ibid.
12. Ibid.
13. Ibid., VI, 7.
14. Ibid., VI, 6.
15. Ibid., VI, 10. Even Seneca, for whom he had more respect than Varro, was caught in this contradiction that led to a fatal hypocrisy. Seneca was critical of civil theology, says Augustine, but his life was a testament to that which he attacked.

> So neither the laws nor custom instituted anything in the civil theology of a sort to please the gods or conform to truth. But though Seneca was made free, in a sense, thanks to the philosophers, yet because he was a distinguished senator of the Roman people, he worshipped what he rebuked, did what he denounced, invoked what he accused. Philosophy, it is clear, had taught him something important, not to be superstitious as a citizen of the world; yet in support of the laws and customs of men, though he did not take the part of an actor in the theatre, philosophy taught him to imitate that actor in the temple. That was the more reprehensible in that he played his dishonest part in such a way that the people thought that he was acting sincerely, whereas an actor on the stage plays rather to amuse the people than to deceive them by any cheat.

16. Ibid., XIX, 4.
17. Ibid.
18. Ibid.
19. Ibid.
20. Ibid.
21. Ibid.
22. Ibid.
23. Ibid., I, 36. See also *Epistles* 91.10 and 29.8.
24. Ibid., II, 6.
25. Ibid.
26. Ibid., II, 7.
27. Ibid., XI, 2.
28. Ibid., I, 22.
29. Ibid.
30. Yves Simon, *A Philosophy of Democratic Government*, Phoenix Books, University of Chicago Press, Chicago, 1951, p. 59.
31. Ibid., p. 34.
32. Wilks, p. 510.

CHAPTER 7

The Origins of Rome and the Dilemmas of Leadership

The city as a whole committed the murder that as a whole it over-looked, so that this way it slew, not its brother, but its father which is worse.

DCD, III, 6

Born in fratricide, nurtured on deception, Rome was constantly threatened with social disintegration. Augustine, of course, felt that no human society could avoid the threat of disorder, but he argued that Rome was particularly ill-prepared to face any disorder. The issue was simple. Faced with a challenge to domestic harmony, Rome returned to the constituent elements of her initial social fabric. But, in returning to these founding principles, Rome had no choice but to reintroduce violence and deception. The key to Rome's success, Augustine argued, did indeed lie in her origins as a people. Those origins were, however, best described not by the classic virtues that Cato, Cicero, and others extolled, but instead by the fratricide, patricide, manipulation, and cynicism of early leaders and citizens.

There is, then, from the beginning a serious dilemma for the Augustinian theory of leadership applied to the Roman case. He saw, in the founding of any society, principles of social cohesion and order that would inevitably be called upon in time of crisis and disorder. In such times, therefore, Rome would return to principles that had over time both contributed and subverted social cohesion and order.

Still, Augustine was fascinated by the fact that Rome had endured for so many centuries. His account of her history analyzes the sources of her success as well as the problems attendant to following early examples of public leadership and the standards of public virtue that guided them. The threat of total disintegration was so clearly apparent in Augustine's time that it was necessary to examine the underlying causes of social disintegration—those that were to be discerned at the very foundation of the Roman city state.

Founders and Gods

In stories of Romulus, Numa, and the earliest gods and kings of Rome, Augustine discovered both the admirable and the unworthy. He praised Romulus and Remus for establishing "an asylum where any man might seek refuge from guilt," [1] viewing it as an "admirable precedent that in due course was followed in the respect shown to Christ's name." He was, however, quick to remind his audience that the foundation of Rome had been sullied by fratricide. Romulus' goal had been to "boast of power." [2] To share his power with his brother was to limit it and so to limit the extent of his boast. Remus was murdered so that he could attain power worthy of his boast. Much that followed in Roman history, Augustine believed, would be contaminated by this act, insofar as it represented the "lust for dominion" of her leaders and the acquiescence of those whom they led to that lust. In fact, Augustine insists that,

> since the crime should in any case have been dealt with, the city as a whole committed the murder that as a whole it overlooked, so that this way it slew, not its brother, but its father which is worse.[3]

The impiety of early Romans thus extended beyond that of its leaders to all of its citizens. Augustine thus attacks the character of the Roman people and so suggests that one who would change Rome must be concerned with more than the character of Roman leadership. Much like Plato, Augustine judged the character of a leader in terms of his ability "to make a people better who were worse before." [4] It would not be enough to bury Romulus' crime nor to mask it through declaring his divinity. The character of an entire people was, therefore, challenged, for a good part of that which they shared and which defined their collective identity was criminal. Much as the integrity and dignity of the young Augustine had been denied by the errors of his elders— the integrity of Rome as a people had been clouded by this founding act. The challenge to all good leadership—to usher in virtue through instruction and example while demanding enough under the best of circumstances—is far greater when a passion for dominion marks the founding of society. Rome's leaders and citizens, Augustine argued, were therefore destined to encounter grave difficulties as they matured as a people.

The division of the earthly city against itself is thus dramatically illustrated, and the pattern of Roman development is foreshadowed. Relying on the tenuous bonds created by a common enemy or the good fortune of a powerful and just political leader, Romans would never develop a sense of themselves as a people able to act for themselves. The fabric of belief that held them together was based on error. Lust for power defined by Romulus' crime and the people's indifference was not in the end compatible with the social life that is the life of the city.

If a city attempts to deal with internal conflicts by developing a collective "boast of power," it may temporarily seem a city of virtue. That is, it may seem to have a sense of collective responsibility. In reality, it is doing little more than revelling in the glory of individual leaders and so masking dissension and conflict. It will, in fact, soon be driven to imperialism and to further external justification of its identity. Looking to an external enemy to provide apparent internal unity, it treated only the symptoms of internal disorder and so risked further civil strife at the conclusion of imperial conquest. This imperialistic dilemma may in turn hide an even more fundamental problem for Roman leadership. There is, it would seem, an inherent contradiction between the public fact of Roman society, the collective boast, and the real aim—an individual boast fulfilled by individual achievements. Often those achievements were those of heroic individuals engaged in battle far from the sight of the Roman citizenry, and far from the domestic faction and conflict always straining to release their divisive energies.

In their pursuit of glory, Roman leaders and citizens had neglected the most basic questions of social harmony and public belief. To be sure, questions of public belief were introduced early in Roman history. Numa Pompilius is praised by Augustine as a religious lawgiver who "established among the Romans many religious institutions." [5] These institutions were not, however, able to confront the self-deception at the foundation of Roman social and political order. Rather, they added a new layer of deception—conscious and explicit deception—to the old. The religious laws of Numa were not instruments of public instruction designed to promote civic virtue. On the contrary, Numa himself, who had unlawfully penetrated the secrets of the demons, had written them down, not for the people but for his own illumination. Augustine comments that,

> he did not dare to teach these things to anyone, nor yet to dispose of
> them by destroying the book or by using them up in any way. It was a
> thing he did not choose to let anyone know for fear of teaching men
> abominable secrets; but he was afraid to tamper with it lest he should
> thereby anger the demons.[6]

Numa's reign was a peaceful one, but it failed to address the dilemma of a social harmony secured by deception. Roman senators who
later discovered Numa's book continued his deception. Burning his
books that they judged to be pernicious, "they considered it the lesser
evil that men should continue their error without knowing the causes
rather than by learning the causes bring turmoil to the State." [7]

Myths of founders, priests, and wise men were maintained in Rome,
not so much because they were believed, but because they were the
social cement of a growing empire. Indeed, Augustine argues, none
save a "small and infant Rome" ever believed Romulus a god. In the
beginning that belief had been the product "not of any *love of . . . error*
but . . . by an *error of love*" [8] (emphasis added). The problem for
Augustine and for the people of Rome was that after the error was
discovered, it was perpetuated. The love that had at one time drawn
them to stories of Romulus had been degraded, leading them to worship false gods. That worship not only did not assist the people, but
instead it increased their oppression. The truth was veiled by "decep-
tive cloaks and fraudulent whitewashings" so that Rome might grow in
dominion and empire.[9]

Cato argued that Rome had lost the virtues that made her great—
"hard work at home and a just rule abroad and in counsel a free spirit,
incapable of crime or yielding to lust." Augustine agreed that things
had grown progressively worse, but insisted that Cato's discussion of
the past was an unwarranted romanticization. He cites Sallust as a
counterauthority, stressing that the powerful had ruled unjustly from
the beginning. The arrogance and lack of public spirit decried by Cato
was a well-established fact, even in the earliest accounts of Roman
history that Augustine had studied. It may well have been that "the
republic in its turn by its very size supplied the means for the vices of
its generals and counsels," but a far more serious deficiency underlay
their disorder.[10] There were not available, in Augustine's terms, standards against which to measure public virtue and thus there was no
public virtue as a practical, operational standard in Roman society.

Even during periods in which just law is partially received, fear
rather than love of justice was the source of Roman unity.[11] The record
of the early days of the republic was one of savage treatment of the
people, high interest rates, double burdens of taxation, and military

service in constant wars. Indeed, Augustine concludes, that what Sallust says of equitable and just law was true "only in comparison to other times, during which morals were certainly worse, inasmuch as factions were more violent." [12] Rome, Augustine insists, never overcame her actual founding principles—violence and deception.

It was critical for Augustine that people remember the sin and the pain of these early times. Augustine had to return to the sins and the pains of youth in order to overcome or at least to confront them and so be more free and whole. In much the same way, a city could begin to free itself only after it had first remembered and so then became able to "overcome past sins and punishments." [13] In each case, Augustine worried that the past must be fully exposed lest its unconscious hold on the present be sustained. It was not sufficient for an individual nor a city merely to forget knowledge of the past through neglect of learning. It was necessary that the past be "experienced and suffered," if in fact individuals and cities were to be "free from the distress" attendant to past evils.[14]

Leadership and Prosperity—The Problem of Roman Success

Those who were charged with sustaining Roman public order were given a difficult task indeed. They were asked to comprehend and to govern an ever more complex empire and at the same time required to forget the experience and the suffering upon which expansion had been built. New experience and new suffering could be accounted for only if they resulted in success on the battlefield.

The Roman cause had been more honorable, says Augustine, when, "energetic at home and in the field [they] made haste, got ready, rallied one another, faced the enemy, and hedged with arms their liberty, their fatherland and their parents." [15] But the Roman people were guilty of misconstruing their victories, coveting them at the expense of higher good—justice and *caritas*. "The inevitable consequence will be new misery and more and more added to the old." [16] Conquest became an end in itself. Standards of public virtue, such as they were, fluctuated from battle to battle.

The inevitable result of this process was the expansion of Rome. Untreated social ills that were a part of the foundation of the city grew apace. It was hard enough for Roman leaders to maintain order in a small unit. With expansion, the problems often seemed unmanageable. Augustine compares the problems of Rome's size to that of the human body, noting that it is

> better to have moderate proportions and have good health than to attain to some gigantic size with never-ending distresses, and where you attain it, secure no peace but be afflicted with ailments that are greater in proportion to the greater size of your members.[17]

Like the Greeks, Augustine worried about the size of a political unit. He agreed as well that size alone would not determine the quality of a city nor of any social unit. Rome's problems were exacerbated by her rapid growth, but they clearly predated that growth. He had argued in Book I of his *Confessions* that the games—and sins—of youth are later repeated by kings and magistrates.[18] In the *City of God* he suggests that Rome's infancy and youth mark the beginning of an educational process that kings and consuls would follow naturally in Rome's young adulthood.[19] Roman leaders had to govern ever larger and diverse peoples, all the while lacking standards of leadership and public virtue needed to bring harmony and order to a much smaller unit.

The real test for Roman leaders and their principles of leadership would occur "when little by little alarms subsided." With war less of a burden, the apparent unity that had grown in response to a common enemy proved to be superficial at best. They were faced with sustaining a public order, but less able, because of the absence of a state of crisis, to depend upon automatic obedience.

> Roman patricians reduced the plebians to the condition of slavery: they disposed of the lives and persons of the plebs in the manner of the kings: they drove men from their lands: and, with the rest of the people disenfranchised, they alone wielded supreme power.[20]

A leader's ability to sustain allegiance to any regime would be challenged in a time of relative peace and order. Roman leaders faced a particularly demanding task under such circumstances as a result of the character of the commitment of ordinary citizens to the Roman state. That commitment was always subject to the shifting winds of opinion and the transient effect of this or that heroic example. One should not, therefore, be surprised at the actions of these early patricians.

These problems were, moreover, not limited to any one period of Roman history. Rome's leaders had always to worry about those times when the Roman people felt secure. The emptiness of her original collective boast of power was revealed in the joylessness of early Republican victories. People were kept restless with temptations to submit to new hardships, not alert to the cycle of victory and despair that accompanied the "specious allurements" of their leaders. Even Cato *"feared security as the enemy of unstable minds* and saw that *fear* was indispensable to the citizens to serve, as it were, *as guardian of their immaturity"*[21] (emphasis added).

Augustine worried about political analysis of this sort, but he understood and knew it to be correct within the context of Roman political ideals as well as Roman political practice. He did not expect that any people would escape temptation, and he knew that disorder and conflict were inevitable in the *saeculum*. It was, furthermore, natural that any leader in the process of maintaining order and fulfilling the day-to-day tasks of his office would lose sight of the formative principles of his society. Leaders and followers of all societies would from time to time find themselves in a position where those principles of social harmony that were advanced at the founding of their society grew dim and uncertain. All of this Augustine knew was a part of the human condition. His hope was that at least a partial remedy could be found for a leader and a people who found themselves falling too far away from those constitutive principles that had defined them in the first place. But, he reasoned, such a plea for renewal depended upon those to whom the renewal was directed and that spirit that was to be revived. Rome faced a dual problem in this regard. First it was not always easy to define a Roman people, to discover those principles or those objects that they shared or loved in common. Second, and more importantly, those principles or objects that Roman leaders and citizens might attempt to revive offered little solace to one who sought to establish or reestablish a regime based on equity and justice.

Leaders of the early republic were in some ways aware of the first, but not the second of these problems of instability. In times of crisis, they had made provision for a temporary dictatorship that would call citizens and leaders together in a flurry of renewed commitment. Military success and the heroic achievement of extraordinary individuals would in turn provide the basis for a newly strengthened civic bond. Rome had, it appears, endorsed Augustine's pessimistic description of human nature. But they failed to understand that the Roman heroic ideal was not an appropriate antidote to those maladies of the human condition that most concerned him. In the end, that ideal actually made those maladies all the more difficult to treat, and so the establishment of equity and justice even less likely.

Times of Crisis and the Roman Heroic Ideal

Unlike the coward, the hero sought glory, honor, and power by an honest path. Using virtuous means to attain those ends, he eschewed the deceitful cunning of the coward and was worthy of some considerable praise.[22] Still, Augustine is cautious in his praise, mindful that there are limits to such virtue. Though heroes are less vile than most men, he comments, they are not appropriate models.

The passion for glory that motivated even the honest man was in fact a vice. It may be that for "one vice, that is the love of praise, [Roman heroes] overcame the love of money and many other vices." [23] Still, it was a vice, for its aim, no matter how artfully veiled, was individual glory and not the good of the commonwealth.[24] The contradiction between the apparent collective boast of power of Roman citizens and the individual boast of the leader is never more apparent. Basking in the reflected glory of the hero, Roman citizens might feel a temporary glow, but they grew, in the process, all the more dependent upon his extraordinary achievements.

The passion for glory and the heroism it spawned had been born in freedom, "but once [Roman heroes] had freedom, so great was the passion for glory that arose, that liberty seemed too little by itself unless they were also seeking dominion over others." [25] That dominion was, of course, explicit and clear when it was the result of foreign conquest. Its domestic victims, though less explicit, were no less real.

Thus tainted by its close relationship to the "lust for dominion," the Roman heroic ideal was deficient on many grounds. For the ordinary citizen, heroic action was intimidating, since by definition it was extraordinary. Insofar as the heroic ideal defines the public world for the ordinary citizen, public acts could be viewed all too easily as rare and unusual—the exception and not the rule for most men.

If the problems that the ordinary citizen might have in identifying with such a public order were significant, the questions faced by the potential hero were at least equally perplexing. What were the standards for heroic action? What defined the hero? The answer was clear but unnerving to Augustine—success on the battlefield. An endless and anxious cycle thus ensues for both leader and citizen. Action in defense of Roman virtue was all too easily circumscribed by military victory. The need to succeed at any cost necessarily came to dominate, because destruction of the very fabric of Roman society was implicit in failure.[26]

Augustine believed that all Roman leadership was to one degree or another based upon deception. He worried, therefore, that leaders, afraid to expose their own deception, would naturally seek a dramatic example to further mask the latent instability of their regimes. One who would challenge the basis of this deception must then challenge the leadership and strengthen the citizenry at the same time. It takes a special kind of strength to confront and overcome the temptations of deception.

The Roman hero might raise himself above the crudest attempts at deception and even successfully challenge the manipulative leader, but Augustine insisted that this was only half of the task. He had, in addition, to provide some kind of direction—social and political education—to an enthralled citizenry.[27] Of this he was incapable. An heroic deed might catch the eye of the citizen, but it could not do more than enthrall him again. The ultimate goal was the creation of "a good will and a right love" and the strength to freely judge between men who would deceive them and men who would lead them to free themselves.[28]

Rome had lost a pious regard for virtue. Augustine sought not simply to restore that piety but to encourage true piety, whereby people could critically judge the defects of their society and develop an alternative to them.[29] It was not enough simply to despise glory and to ignore the opinions of fickle crowds. Augustine's effort to free his reader entailed more than simple opposition to Rome.

For Augustine, judgment truly becomes possible only as individuals become capable of comprehending the consequences of their judgments. This was the case, he argued in his *Confessions,* with children as they passed through adolescence and into young adulthood, and so it was with a people who would be responsible for its own actions. Left without the tradition and guidance of a just social order, Roman people lacked the public standards necessary to exercise their freedom in a public world. Freedom was defined as the opposite of the oppression of a king like Tarquin.[30] Such freedom was no more useful to Roman citizens than was Augustine's rebellious freedom as a boy. It became an unbridled and post hoc rebellion against such rule rather than the basis of an alternative. Augustine had seen this in the early days of the Republic, just as he remembered it in his own childhood. He longed for someone to regulate Rome's disorders much as he had for his personal disorders.

Augustine sought to develop "freedom of judgment," as noted in detail in Chapter 2.[31] The standards of judgment offered by Rome in fact frustrated that freedom and instead promoted a "calculus of pleasure." Appeals to Roman citizenry might be cloaked in patriotic garb, but in the end they were directed not to the "rationality of the thoughtful man" but to the "one who is ruled by desire."[32] Roman standards of value thus led not to freedom and public virtue but to an implicit denial of the latter and a frustration of the former. Augustine's critique of Rome was in fact a critique of antipolitics. His alternative awaits the articulation of new standards of value and new men capable of freedom of judgment.

He appreciated the valor of men like Cato on the one hand, and bemoaned the lack of good public administrators on the other.[33] But his analysis pushed beyond concern with formal and structural problems. In fact—as we have seen—much of his attack on Rome centered on its excessive formalism. Who are the men who will fill the positions and, more important, what are their principles, he asked? Men had to learn to recognize substantive differences among those who would lead them. Lacking a strong foundation upon which the bonds of social and political unity were established, Roman heroes and leaders were in grave difficulty. There were, however, other civilizations that, for Augustine, offered different standards of leadership and models of integrity and self-respect for his people.

Notes

1. *DCD*, I, 34.
2. Ibid., XV, 5.
3. Ibid., III, 6.
4. Gorgias, 515d. in Plato, *The Collected Dialogues*, E. Hamilton and H. Cairns, eds., Princeton, Princeton University Press, 1969. See also *DCD*, II, 20; V, 19 and V, 24.
5. *DCD*, VII, 34.
6. Ibid.
7. Ibid.
8. Ibid., XXII, 6. The paradox here is striking. Romans acquired an empire partly because of a misconceived faith—an "error of love"—in the divinity of the gods, Romulus in particular. But the empire once acquired becomes the reason for maintaining beliefs now thought to be in error. A total inversion is evident for secular men whom Augustine saw destined to these unanticipated and literally perverse consequences.
9. Ibid. Herbert Deane has suggested in response to this argument that all peoples, with the exception of Israel, are founded in comparable ways. Whatever the historical accuracy of this assertion, Augustine's use of Israel as a counterexample retains its educational force. While he understands the exceptional nature of Israel, he uses the virtuous endeavors of her citizens to suggest to late Roman citizens the possibility of a more just— though surely not perfect—society.
10. Ibid.
11. Ibid., II, 18. Of course, Augustine sees the utility of fear as an element in holding any social group together. As we have seen, however, he insisted that one must go well beyond fear, if a common association based on the general interest were to be established and maintained.
12. Ibid., III, 16.
13. Ibid., XXII, 30.
14. It is important to note, as Herbert Deane has reminded me, that Augustine speaks here of the eternal city not of any earthly city. Indeed no earthly city could ever be totally free, nor could any individual. His teaching here, as it was in his *Confessions,* aims at a margin of freedom and judgment. Though perfection is impossible, he suggests that both individuals and

cities can be more free and so more capable of exercising judgment than they were under the dominion of Rome. See *Confs.*, I, 14; VIII, 8; IX, 1; *DCD*, V, 9, and also *Ep.*, 91.6 and *Ep.*, 138.V.17.

15. Ibid., III, 10.
16. Ibid., XV, 4.
17. Ibid., III, 10.
18. *Confs.*, I, 19.
19. *DCD*, XVI, 43.
20. Ibid., III, 17. This "long period of years up to the Second Punic War" was symptomatic of the troubles faced by Rome in time of peace.
21. Ibid., I, 30.
22. *DCD*, V, 12.
23. Ibid., V, 13.
24. The true good of the commonwealth and the will of God are, of course, parallel here. As the will of God is ignored, so is the good of the commonwealth. See, for example, *Ep.*, 91.
25. *DCD*, V. 13.
26. *DCD*, IV, 32. In Rome "men who posed as prudent and wise made it their business to deceive the people in matters of religion." Augustine continues:

> In this they not only worship, but also imitate the demons, whose greatest desire is to deceive. For just as demons can only possess those whom they have treacherously deceived, so also the rulers—certainly not honest men, but men like demons—taught the people as true in matters of religion what they knew to be false. In this way they bound them with tighter chains, as it were, to the civil society, in order that they might possess men similarly enthralled. Now what weak and untaught person could at the same time escape the deception of the rulers and that of the demons.

> One who would challenge the basis of this deception must then challenge the leadership and strengthen the citizenry at the same time, for it takes a special kind of strength to confront and overcome the temptations of deception.

27. *DCD*, IV, 32. See note 25.
28. Ibid., XI, 16.
29. Ibid., V. 19, 20. Roman self-satisfaction, Augustine insists, is a dangerously false one. The first danger was that men would become the simpering slaves of the praise of other men, acting not out of concern for public virtue but reacting through the blush of their own vanity. Yet men may be trapped another way if—having recognized the hollowness of parasitic praise—they turn solely to internal standards of judgment:

> And yet men must not think to free themselves from this degradation by posing as despisers of glory and paying no heed to the opinions of others, while they esteem themselves as wise men and win their own approval. For their virtue, if it exists, is dependent on the praise of man in another kind of way. For the man who wins his own approval is still a man. But he who with genuine piety believes in God and hopes in him, is more concerned about what he finds displeasing in himself than what (if anything) is pleasing, not so much to himself as to the Truth.

The public order—God's order—can no more be served this way than through a more direct reliance on glory and reputation as guides.

30. Ibid., XI, 16. Such freedom, says Augustine, was illusory. He seeks true freedom; he says freedom "which makes men free from the tyranny of sin and death and the devil" *(DCD,* V, 18). If men would seek freedom—the freedom to act—they must look beyond escape from physical oppression (however important that may be) and confront the cultural and psychological tyrannies that have prepared the way for tyrannical rule in the first place. "Our motive," he suggests, "is not a passion for the praise of men, but a love that would set men free, not from King Tarquin, but from demons and the prince of demons."
31. Ibid.
32. Ibid.
33. Ibid., V, 12.

CHAPTER EIGHT

The Covenantal Origins
of Old Testament Leadership

*For there is not true virtue except that which aims at the goal where
the good of man is found, the good that has no better.*

DCD, V, 12

The Old Testament served many purposes for Augustine—the
teacher. Through the stories of the Old Testament, he introduces a new
history and a new triad of leaders. The history of the people of God
was at once older and more virtuous than that of Rome. Old Testament
leaders, turning to that history and to those people, constantly educated
and, in times of crisis, renewed their society in a way that was not
available to Roman leaders. These stories not only begin the history of
the city of God, but they have as well an independent force for Augustine. His craftsman's sense leads him to compare and contrast Rome
to Assyria, Babylon, and Israel, as well as to Christian society. In addition, his sense of the difficulty of introducing the mysteries of Christianity leads him naturally to the stories of the Old Testament. In the
City of God, as he had earlier in his *Confessions,* Augustine begins his
teaching with the concrete—the material—and proceeds very slowly to
the spiritual, as he attempted to mediate between the finitude of men's
experiences and the infinity that was God.

Augustine argues that early promises to the people of God, the
promises of God to the people of the Old Testament, were "promises

of earthly gifts." The new covenant, in contrast, promised the Kingdom
of Heaven. The Old Testament "gave the appearance of containing
promises of carnal things." [1] The need for these promises would in time
be overcome as spiritual desires and rewards dominated. All of this was
set out in God's two promises to Abraham.

> One indeed, is that his deed should possess the land of Canaan, and this
> is indicated by the words: "Go into the land that I shall show you, and I
> will make of you a great nation." But the other is much more notable,
> since it refers not to his carnal but to his spiritual seed, by which he is
> father not alone of the people of Israel, but of all peoples who follow in
> the footsteps of his faith. And this promise was first made in these words
> "And in you shall all the tribes of the earth be blessed." [2]

The second promise, however important to the history of the city of
God on earth, was not a central part of the story of Abraham. The first
pledge in fact was fulfilled over time, as Judges replaced Moses and
Joshua, and the people of Abraham settled in Israel. The second pledge
would be fulfilled by Christ in the flesh, not by the observance of the
old law but by faith in the gospel. The true significance of that faith
could not, however, be understood without careful comparison and
contrast of Christianity to both Rome and Israel, to the character of the
people of Rome and the people of Abraham.

Augustine's own craft is clearly at work as he retells these stories.
Again, as in his *Confessions,* he prepares his readers, even as he speaks
of the preparatory endeavors of others. The founding generations of
leaders from Abraham to Moses prepare their people for more mature,
rational judgment in much the way that Augustine himself had attempted to prepare the readers of his *Confessions* for more mature
judgment as they turned, after reading them, to the scriptures. The
stories of the Old Testament—though stories of godly people—serve to
mediate between his account of the history of Rome and the mysteries
of Christian faith. In contrast to his *Confessions,* Augustine presented
stories of the maturation of an entire people in the *City of God.* He
hoped that just as the people of the Old Testament had passed to even
more mature judgment, his people in the fifth century A.D. might more
successfully learn to judge the righteousness of those who would lead
them.

Patriarchs and Shepherds

Through the story of Cain and Abel, Augustine sharply distinguishes
the founding traditions of the people of the Old Testament from those

of Rome. He notes that Cain and Abel were not envious of one another after the fashion of Romulus and Remus, "for Abel did not want
power in the city that was being founded by his brother." Indeed
Cain's fratricide was more diabolical than that of Romulus in that the
envy that drove him to murder was based on the envy that "the wicked
feel for the good." [3] Cain's envy foreshadows the most basic problem
of the city of man, for it attacks the very foundation of peace and
social harmony. Goodness, he argues

> is a possession of the undifferentiated love of fellow-members; and the
> more harmony there is among men, the further that possession extends.
> Consequently, anyone who refuses to share this possession with another
> will not have it at all; and he will find that the extent of his possession of
> it is in proportion to his success in loving a partner in it.[4]

Cain's earthly city has been set in dramatic contrast to the life of Yahweh's favorite. The argument between Cain and Abel had a more fundamental source than the tension born of human weakness. It was
symbolic of the eternal and desperate conflict between the city of man
and the city of God.

There are two lessons—one general and one specific—presented here.
First, the distinction between absolute good and evil is introduced as a
general educational device through which Augustine hoped to force
men to confront their own weakness. The sharp polarity noted in the
story of Cain and Abel—unreal at most times and places—placed in
relief real principles of ordinary social life that had been glossed over
by custom, law, the desire for praise, and other human faults that
dominated the culture of Rome and most other earthly cities. In the
second place, he introduces here the possibility of a genuine and lasting
social harmony.

Although the social life of the city is to be desired, it cannot be
presumed. For Augustine, the Classical world was fraught with examples of such presumption. The biblical world offered him examples not
of perfection but of the pursuit of peace and justice. Still, there were
positive examples of what people could accomplish.

Cain's fratricide put the task of biblical leadership in dramatic relief.
The wickedness of the earthly city was more basic than even the envy
and pride that it encouraged. New categories of analysis and judgment
had to be discovered, if one was to confront this evil. Augustine presented an example of the use of these new categories in his own analysis of Rome. The basis of that analysis—the source of the new
categories—could now be examined more directly. From the beginning
of the eleventh book, he argued that men must look for renewal to the
True Founder of human society.

The Founder of the city of God is, of course, the God of Genesis, whose actions we are "enjoined to accept . . . on faith." He is the "craftsman, creator, and founder" of our world,[5] and he is unlike other craftsmen who give form to physical substances, such as potters and smiths. He is a creator and founder, unlike Romulus and Alexander "by whose will, plan and power" Rome and Alexandria were built.[6] The will, plan, and power of God are superior to those of any mortal, but the significance of human authority and leadership should not be undervalued. Indeed, the Old Testament, especially in Augustine's account, is the story of the founding of an earthly nation. The possibility of that founding is sustained, first by Seth and then by Noah, who was "perfect in his generation, that is, perfect, not as the citizens of the City of God are to become, but as they can be during their sojourn here on earth."[7] Noah's craftsmanship and leadership is, however, preliminary to another human act—Abraham's show of obedience, righteousness, and faith.

Abraham signals, for Augustine, a new era, literally a turning point of time, in which the evidence for the city of God becomes more explicit.[8] During his lifetime, mortal men witness the creation of that chosen people who would mature into a great nation. Leaving the house of his father, Abraham becomes himself a father—the father of a nation. It would be ruled not by human standards but by faith in the obedience to God. It was a nation for which Abraham, through his obedience and faith, would establish the foundation. "Abraham underwent temptation in regard to the sacrifice of his beloved son Isaac," says Augustine, "to the end that his devoted obedience might be put to the proof and be brought to the attention of later ages, not of God."[9] His was a personal trial of strength through which he arrived at self-knowledge—knowledge of strength as well as his limitations. His personal trial would be extended to a collective one, during which his people—following his example—would gain knowledge of themselves. His personal example and his leadership served to direct his people through the years of their adolescence as a people to prepare them for the responsibilities of young adulthood as a settled nation.

Abraham's role as a mediator was to keep God's requirements before his people, reminding them that the social unity they had forged would be regularly challenged by those who found these demands too burdensome. He attempted to sustain their quest toward unity in the face of external and internal attacks, while insisting that smaller units are preferable to that universal rule that requires force. The psychological motivation is similar to that developed in Augustine's *Confessions*. Abraham's dependence on God was a constant reminder of his own limits, and it prevented him from becoming either totally self-reliant or overly self-satisfied. This awareness taught Abraham that leadership could never be complacent, but must always be consciously acting and reaffirming. Augustine found in Abraham's successors a faith that renews the spirit of a people through the understanding of obedience to both their patriarch and God. These shepherds led their flocks with constant reminders of the special authority of both their heavenly founder and their earthly founder and father—Abraham. The authority of each shepherd was reaffirmed by his people in the common acceptance of their origins as a people. They had passed through infancy in the period of time from Adam to Noah and then through a period resembling children from Noah to Abraham.[10] During this time, they learned to communicate with one another, much as children did. Then, during the period from Abraham to David, the Israelites gained a sense of responsibility for one another and came to understand their obligations to their neighbors. Only then, Augustine suggests, were they prepared to assume the burdens of governance. God's promises would be fulfilled, but not until his people had learned the magnitude of the task that lay before them.

The culmination of this great founding task was led by Moses. Having been given a law that bound the people to God and to one another more explicitly than had God's covenant with their earthly father, these people were challenged to wander for forty years in the wilderness under Moses' leadership. Augustine is careful to distinguish the leadership of Moses from other earthly leaders—specifically Lycurgus. Moses' legitimacy was signalled by miracles witnessed by all. Moses' role as one of the founders of Israel is even more clearly established than was that of Lycurgus in Sparta.

"The true education of the human race," Augustine noted, "was like that of an individual, it advanced by steps in time, as the individual's does when a new stage in life is reached." [11] It mounted, as did Augustine's teaching, "from the level of temporal things to a level where it could grasp the eternal and from visible things to a grasp of invisibles." [12] The task of each of the patriarchs was to prepare for that future, even as they established the foundation for temporal order and instructed their followers through the use of visible things.

The system of belief that would become the social cement of Abraham's people was a part of its founding tradition. The contrast with Rome was obvious and crucial to Augustine's educational mission. Shared belief in this society was not imposed after the fact, as though somehow external to the creation of the basic social unit.[13] On the contrary, the covenant that granted Abraham his authority created a people, for it had given them a common object of love that they could freely and openly accept. Even more important, however, was the nature of that object, for implicit in the love of God was a "love of fellow members" that substantively reaffirmed their commonality. As Augustine suggests:

> If, however, the Creator should be truly loved, that is if he himself should be loved and not something else in his stead which is not he, he cannot be loved in a bad way. For we *must* observe due order in loving even the love itself with which we love in a good way what is worthy of love, if there is to be in use the virtue that enables us to live a good life. Hence, in my opinion, a short and true definition of virtue is "a rightly ordered love." [14]

Again there is a unity of theory and practice. The affirmation of this covenant, and so of a common love of God, required a specific set of behaviors and attitudes without which the covenant would be invalid and common love denied.

Rome, too, recognized the formal importance of a founding tradition. She had, however, manipulated that tradition not in the common interest but in the interest of prideful individuals that divided the nation.

> The Roman people is a people, and its estate is without doubt a state. But what this people loved in its early and in subsequent times, and by what moral decline it passed into bloody sedition and then into social and civil warfare, and disrupted and corrupted that very unity of heart, which is, so to speak, the health of a people, history bears witness. . . .[15]

This was then a people that set about destroying its own unity as a people. Roman founding traditions never in practice realized their aims, for they never overcame pride. Theirs was an "error of love." [16] Augustine's theory of leadership was directed toward overcoming this error through providing a more worthy focus for common attachment and love.

Judges and Kings

God's promise was even more concretely fulfilled after the death of Moses. Joshua then "governed the people and led them into the land of promise and divided it among them." [17] The character of Roman rule in contrast to that of the people of God is here clearly apparent. As the people settle, judges and kings appeared to guide them, and formal political institutions were established. Unlike their Roman counterparts, however, these leaders and their institutions were not characterized by a lust for power that dominated Roman leaders and the nations they subjugated.[18] The judges and kings of Israel, though influenced by carnal temptations, resided in a nation whose spirit was much closer to that of the heavenly city in which "both those put in charge and those placed under them served one another in love, the former by their counsel, the latter by their obedience." [19]

David, as noted earlier, was for Augustine the pivotal figure here. His rule exemplified much that Augustine found worthy in the people of the Old Testament. Indeed, David initiates a new order. His people had passed through their "adolescence" and had found their identity in a common love of God. They had now to act upon that identity and sustain it. David's piety was such that both he and his people were able to endure the temptations attendant to success in any earthly city or nation. All were tested, but the living memory of Abraham's covenant with God continued to dominate and guide their judgments. Indeed, Augustine notes that "fulfillment came under David and his son Solomon, whose dominion was extended over the whole area mentioned in the promise." [20]

Insofar as rulers and ruled piously obeyed the law and so respected their covenant with God, their worldly territory was sustained. Disobedience and impiety were, however, inevitable. Temporal punishments were imposed to help train those who fell away from the law, but even these were inadequate. The development into "young manhood" brought with it a new challenge to Old Testament leaders. Patriarchs and shepherds had done their work in forming the substance of a people—their belief, their common experience. It was now left to the kings to sustain it in a time of prosperity. Just as Augustine had warned the individual of the dangers of complacency in his *Confessions,* he looked, in the *City of God,* to the book of Samuel to suggest that a whole people could also become complacent. Leaders had constantly to confront the reality of temptation.

Successful rule created prosperity, and the attention of the society was diverted from the most important of social and political questions.[21] Quickly forgetting more trying times, men sought security and peace. Having lost an appreciation for the nature of the "foundation of the world" and of their own kingdom, they risked losing the ability to "execute judgment and righteousness." Their founding covenant ignored, their very identity as a people was threatened and so, of course, was the continuing stability of their nation.[22] Without this focus of common agreement, they could no longer be a people and so, says Augustine, God intervened.

> In the end, as his indignation increased, that whole nation was not only crushed in its own territory by the Chaldean army but was also for the most part deported into the lands of the Assyrians, first that part which was called Israel, consisting of ten tribes, and later Judah also, when Jerusalem and its temples of such renown had been overthrown.[23]

Augustine teaches important lessons here. The founding tradition offers a people something important to hold in common and thus grants them their very status as a people. If, however, that which they hold in common is lost—no matter how strong it was in the beginning—the results are disastrous. Knowing well the perils of success and prosperity, Augustine saw the Old Testament prophet as one who attempted to remind men of their covenantal responsibilities.

Prophetic Judgment

"In the Christian view of history," suggests Sheldon Wolin, "there was no place for *fortuna,* by the same logic none for the political hero." [24] Similarly, Augustine viewed the hero as inimical to Christian society. Nonetheless, Augustine and the biblical history he interprets faced periods of crisis in which the established leaders were found unable to "execute judgment and righteousness." Periods of this sort called for men of exceptional talent. For Augustine, the problem with the Roman hero was that he reflected the very crisis he was confronting. Lacking the vision of distance and perspective, these men, he insisted, failed to reinject the judgment sorely needed by the society. Augustine sees the Old Testament prophets filling this void in a way that the Roman hero could not.

The special skill of the prophet was his "judgment on the meaning of his experience." [25] Whether his vision was of public facts—available to everyone or of things hidden and accessible only to his own mind—the prophet offered an interpretation of his experience that reaffirmed the existence of a greater order through which men might reexamine the experiences that had led them to crisis. He might offer a source of new strength to the "mind of man, the natural seat of his reason and understanding, weakened by long standing faults which darken it." When that mind had become too weak to cleave to that experience and enjoy God's eternal light, someone was needed who could direct people towards renewal and health.[26]

The prophet could perform this task in a way that Old Testament kings, blinded by more immediate difficulty, could not. The therapeutic concerns of the Augustine of the *Confessions* have thus clearly been expanded. Roman social and political identity, tenuous at best for most people, forced Augustine in his *Confessions* to begin the job of building community from the bottom up. The Old Testament prophet, by contrast, could rely on a preexisting community and a corresponding social and political identity. Prophetic teaching therefore, offers not only a link between the testaments but a clue as to the sort of moral/political education that Augustine admires within the framework of an ongoing society.

Augustine thought prophecy to be central to the entire biblical tradition. Indeed, by the time he wrote the *City of God,* he had come to think of prophecy and the scriptures as nearly synonomous. Once again, however, Augustine's craftsmanship led him to use prophetic stories in more than one fashion. He notes in fact that "the utterances of the prophets are found to have a threefold meaning in that some have in view the earthly Jerusalem, others the heavenly, and others refer to both." [27] In the present context, our concern is with the first use of prophecy and with the contrast between the prophetic tradition on the one hand and the heroic tradition on the other. The latter may from time to time speak of virtue, but it does so without knowing the true foundation of virtue. Neither philosophers nor heroes offered reliable witness of the foundation of public virtue, for they were all ignorant "of the goals and the standards by which all of these [virtues] were to be judged." [28]

Roman concern for public virtue belied a tradition that looked to the glory of the individual. The Old Testament tradition, aided here by the prophet, sought to reunite public and private goods through Yahweh's covenant with Abraham and the virtue that it taught—"a rightly ordered love." These were not lessons, Augustine noted, "inculcated by embattled words." [29]

The role of the prophet had been fundamental "from the time when the people of Israel . . . began to have kings. . . ." [30] They appeared to remind and renew. The covenantal foundation of society—the basis of their faith and of their nation—was reintroduced at regular intervals through divine inspiration, the inspiration again of virtue, of rightly ordered love that was made known to those whose loves had become disordered. The prophetic task (somewhat mechanically represented below) was to reestablish contact between ongoing social and political affairs and the founding principles that had given social substance to those affairs.

	Rome	Israel
Founder	Romulus	Abraham
Renewer	Hero	Prophet
Stabilizer	Kings	Kings

When comparable men had attempted to act in Rome, their efforts were set in a morass of contradiction. Cato, whom Augustine clearly admired, had attempted to warn of disaster and to turn men back to founding principles. In Augustine's terms, he faced grave difficulties, for those very principles threatened the pursuit of a truly public virtue. Cato himself could not escape a world dominated by human glory.

> Glory, honour and power, which the Romans desired above all, the goal to which their good men climbed by good arts, should not bring virtue in its train, but they should follow virtue. For there is not true virtue except that which aims at the goal where the good of man is found, the good that has no better. Hence Cato ought not even to have sought the honours that he sought; rather, the state should have granted them to reward his virtue without his seeking them.[31]

Cato was trapped by the culture in which he lived. The foundation to which he turned was not that of a healthy people, and he was infected by the same diseases that festered in others.

Because of the relative health of his society, the prophet escaped many of these difficulties. He thus became in Augustine's account a significant leadership force, facing crisis with personal integrity and consistency, reminding men of the very nature of social harmony and peace. His attempts might be frustrated, but they were not self-contradictory. The possibility of such prophetic intervention was critically important to Augustine's theory of leadership and to his own leadership task. He hoped, as he had in his *Confessions*, that his words would awaken in his fifth-century audience both the possibility of change and an understanding of the basis of change.

Augustine argued, of course, that these prophets also served to foretell the coming of Christ. In fact, he says, those "wellsprings of prophecy [which] gushed forth . . . at the time when the Assyrian empire ended" were timed to coincide with the founding of Rome "which was to rule the nations of the world." [32] Prophecy that had at first "been for the use of [the people of Israel] only" now looked with Rome to the entire world and so as well to the fulfillment of God's second promise [33] to Abraham that he should be a father "to all peoples who follow in the footsteps of his faith."

Augustine thus sees his role as helping to fulfill God's promise to Abraham. He suggests that only a people like the Romans, corrupted as they were by *superbia* and power on a universal scale, could understand the message of Christ. Only such a people had endured over time the hardships resulting from universal error, in opposition to which universal truth begins to be imaginable. The people of the Old Testament had learned much, but their capacity for learning was necessarily limited.

Rome's dominion paved the way for Christ's in that it shifted the focus from the problems of a single nation to those of all people. With the Babylonian captivity came a new stage in the life of the people of God, and a warning that their life was not to be fulfilled in an earthly kingdom. The growing power of Rome demonstrated the folly of man's pretensions to truly just rule. The world of the Old Testament had offered an example of a rule more just than in any period of Roman history, but it too had been subject to that error to which all earthly kings and kingdoms had fallen victim. Augustine, therefore, sees the fulfillment of God's second promise to Abraham, both as an antidote to Rome and a corrective to the errors of the kings and people of the Old Testament.

The character of Roman rule could not be challenged by a single nation nor by the moral and political standards of a single people. If God's people were to survive, they would have to offer an alternative to Roman culture that would awaken in all people the possibility of a new moral-political order. That order was not to be constructed by political craftsmen of the sort that built Rome, Assyria, or even those who had with God's direction founded the nation of Israel. The new order was instead to be ushered in by the instruction provided by a Christian *paideia*.[34] A new moral doctrine, separated from the difficult necessities of structuring and ordering political institutions, had emerged. Augustine developed that doctrine in the service of God for the people of God sojourning on earth and in the *saeculum*.

Notes

1. *DCD*, III, 15 and 25.
2. Ibid., XVI, 16.
3. Ibid., XV, 5.
4. Ibid.
5. Ibid., XII, 4.
6. Ibid., XII, 26.
7. *DCD*, XV, 16 and 26.
8. Ibid., XVI, 12.
9. Ibid, XVI, 31 and 32.
10. Ibid., XVI, 43.
11. Ibid., X, 14.
12. Ibid.
13. Ibid., XXII, 6.
14. Ibid., XV, 22.
15. Ibid., XIX, 24.

16. Ibid., XXII, 6.
17. Ibid., XVI, 43.
18. Ibid., XIV, 28.
19. Ibid.
20. Ibid., XVII, 3.
21. Ibid., XVII, 20. Augustine refers to Sallust in speaking of the dangers of prosperity and in so doing clearly introduces the scope of problems attendant to Solomon's reign. See Sallust, "The Conspiracy of Catiline," 11.8 in *Jurgurthine War/The Conspiracy of Catiline,* Penguin Books, London, 1975, pp. 182–83.
22. Ibid., XVII, 4. Augustine says, for example, that:

    We see also that the earthly Jerusalem, who had many sons, has grown feeble, for whatever sons of the free woman were in the city were her strength, but now since *the letter is alone there, and not the spirit,* her strength has departed and she has become weak (emphasis added).

23. Ibid., XVII, 23.
24. Sheldon Wolin, p. 127.
25. Robert A. Markus, *Saeculum: History and Society in the Theology of Saint Augustine,* Cambridge, Cambridge University Press, 1970, p. 194.
26. *DCD,* XI, 2.
27. Ibid., XVII, 3.
28. Ibid., XVIII, 41.
29. Ibid.
30. Ibid., XVIII, 27.
31. Ibid., V, 12.
32. Ibid., XVIII, 41.
33. Ibid.
34. Eugene Kevane has made the strongest case for Augustine's Christian *paideia.* See, for example, *Augustinian Studies,* Annual Publication of the Augustinian Institute, Villanova University, vol. I, 1970, pp. 164ff.

CHAPTER NINE

Conclusion: Political Education and Christian Leadership

Rome worshipped her founder as a god in a temple when she was already built and dedicated, while our Jerusalem placed its Founder and its God, Christ, in the foundation of faith to the end that it might be built and dedicated.

DCD, XXII, 6

"The New Lawgiver and the Christian Prince"

The birth of Christ transformed all previous approaches to the questions of leadership. "The priesthood and the monarchy were transformed," Augustine suggests, "by the new and eternal priest and king in the single person of Christ Jesus." [1] Previous models were still significant but new directions were now indicated. Augustine could approve Justin Martyr's description of Christ as the "new lawgiver"—the architect of community.[2] Writing His new laws into the minds and hearts of His people, the Creator of a new social force, God directly attacked the tyranny of Roman superstition.[3] Christ too was a founder *(conditor)* but of a very different sort than Romulus.

> Although Christ is the founder of a heavenly and eternal city, his city did not believe in him as God because it was founded by him, but rather it is to be founded because it believes. Rome worshipped her founder as a god in a temple when she was already built and dedicated, while our

Jerusalem placed its Founder and its God, Christ, in the foundation of faith to the end that it might be built and dedicated.[4]

The difference in timing was critical for Augustine. A city he argued, is defined by its citizens, not by its walls.[5] A citizenry defined initially by the walls of the city would, he counselled, be subject to shifting definition as the walls grew and/or contracted. A people such as that of the Old Testament, whose character as a people was defined by a founding covenant, could survive challenges because its internal resources were not primarily dependent upon walls and institutions. Shared belief preceded common love and affection in the case of the heavenly city. Shared belief followed common love and affection in the earthly city. The differences were predictable and in the case of the latter catastrophic.

> The one city, loving its founder, put faith in him as a god; the other believing its founder to be God, gave her love to him. In the same way as Rome's reason for loving came first, and after it her willingness to believe even a false tale to the credit of her beloved, so Jerusalem's reason for believing came first to preserve her by right faith from a rash love of the false and ensure her love of the true.[6]

The potential force of such belief was great, even given the limitations of this life. Christian belief was, for Augustine, all the more powerful as it extended beyond the confines of a single nation. Removed from the restraints of a particular society and its unique social and political institutions, people were given through Christianity a weapon with which to militantly confront the universalistic claims of Rome. Perhaps more significantly, Christianity permitted commitment to social and political justice both apart from and within existing political institutions.

New standards of judgment were here introduced—standards that might allow people to escape from both the folly and rashness of Roman culture and rigid commitment to the letter of Old Testament law as well. Through true belief, and through a rightly ordered love, *caritas* could be realized as a proximate as well as an ultimate end. Augustine saw Christ as a model as well as a teacher—a model directly accessible to Romans and dramatically implicated in their own history. He told his Roman audience "that Jesus is the substance of that people from whom came his birth in the flesh." [7]

"True justice," he maintained, "exists only in that republic whose Founder and Ruler is Christ." This is a republic, for it is without question the "people's estate." [8] Indeed, it is by definition more surely the people's estate, for it is God and the people's belief, love and commitment that created it. They could continue to love truth precisely because their existence as a people was firmly established in their most basic beliefs. Their strength and identity as a people confidently asserted, they could risk careful assessment of truth and falsity. Judgment—powerful collective judgment—was possible only if that identity was secure. In the absence of a secure identity, a people would rush to defend themselves and to define themselves through the actions of their leaders regardless of the merit or justice oɪ those actions. Christianity offered such security. In fact he suggests in a letter written in 412 A.D. that,

> were our religion listened to as it deserves, it would establish, consecrate, strengthen, and enlarge the commonwealth in a way beyond all that Romulus, Numa, Brutus, and all the other men of renown in Roman history achieved. For what is a republic but a commonwealth? Therefore its interests are common to all. . . .[9]

Christian Emperors and Christian Magistrates

For Christian political leaders, whether they be emperor or magistrate, Augustine counselled prudence. That prudence was guided by a vision of social harmony combined with an understanding of the difficulty of ever achieving it. Like Plato and Rousseau, Augustine presents a vision of perfection that mortal men cannot attain. The substance of that vision and the nature of its presentation are, however, meant to influence the character of the lives and institutions of mortal men.[10] Leaders would find it easier to rule in an atmosphere free of Roman flattery and suspicion. All would find peace and harmony easier to sustain.

There are, however, a number of significant and related problems: finding such a Christian ruler, keeping him aware of his responsibilities, and more importantly, educating a people to recognize and respect such a ruler. As Augustine suggests in *De Utilitate Credenti:*

> For in what way shall we fools be able to find a wise man, whereas this name, although hardly anyone dare openly, yet most men lay claim indirectly: so disagreeing with one another in the very matters, in the knowledge of which wisdom consists, as that it must be either none of them, or some certain one be wise? But when the fool inquires, who is the wise man? I do not at all see, in what way he can be distinguished and perceived. For by no signs whatever can one recognize any thing, whereof these are signs.[11]

At first glance, this passage seems to suggest that only the wise could recognize a wise man, but Augustine's argument is more complicated than that. As he made clear through his *Confessions*, he insisted that men were educable and were, therefore, capable of receiving treatment and therapy. Education in self-understanding had now to be supplemented with education in civic virtue. This would not, however, be easy. Public education had become a game that sought not to reaffirm public standards but to teach men to manipulate public opinion. As the skill of the manipulators grew, standards for judging the virtue of their performances receded. Roman education—as Augustine knew from his own experience—had made public virtue the subject of ridicule. How then, he asked, could such standards be reintroduced and who would introduce them?

In a general way, Augustine suggested that certain kinds of rulers are appropriate for certain kinds of people. He made it clear, however, that there is a formative and reformative relationship between the two. A people, for Augustine, is defined in terms of the objects of its love. It is apparent, moreover, that one of the main tasks of a leader of the people is to represent those objects upon which common agreement is based. This, he argued, is surely a significant part of that process of public education that determines the nature of the city. However, he felt that only an institution not contaminated by Roman culture could change the nature of Roman cities.

Augustine spoke of the qualities of Christian magistrates, princes, and emperors, but he believed that earthly regimes were limited and could not be modelled on the heavenly city. Likewise, he attacked chiliasts and millenarians and insisted that any attempt to endow any present or future Christian ruler with messianic or quasi-messianic traits was misguided. The Christian ruler shared the situation of his pagan counterpart. That is, he

> differs from the pagan, not in the amount of power that he wields nor in the nature of the state which he maintains: he differs only in his awareness of where power stands in God's order, to what end it is related and what ends it may serve.[12]

The character of life in the *saeculum* required power wielders. The duty of the Christian leader was thus twofold: first, he must delineate that which was proper to his role and conduct himself justly within those limits. Second, and more important, he must learn to promote a new order of love—a set of standards to follow while executing his still very earthly duties. This second task requires that he encourage the development of leaders and teachers apart from the state. Their counsel and instruction, Augustine hoped, would foster such fellowship and harmony as *caritas* could bring to the *saeculum*.

Augustine addresses each of these responsibilities in the *City of God* when he describes the Christian emperor. His duty to wield power and execute the order of the state is paired with a duty to "spread the worship of God far and wide," and thereby to promote instruction of citizens in the most basic virtues and to make them thereby better citizens.[13] Likewise, the Christian judge is asked to execute justice all the while, maintaining "the duty of an affectionate father" so that the spirit of *caritas* is kept alive even as earthly order is maintained.[14] And so it was with the Christian magistrate, who would have to exercise a "benevolent severity" in correcting men, whose "welfare rather than their wishes it is our duty to consult." [15] He would sustain order and at the same time promote *caritas*.

Far from being incompatible with the state's well-being, the doctrine of Christ promotes the highest virtues of the commonwealth. He writes in a letter in 412 A.D. that if only soldiers and subjects, husbands and wives, parents and children, kings and judges and even taxpayers and tax gatherers obeyed that doctrine, it "would be the salvation of the commonwealth." Christ preached the voluntary practice of "poverty, continence, benevolence, justice and concord" among people as well as true piety. He looked first to eternal salvation, but he also preached that men should have honorable lives in the pursuit of "the most perfect bond of concord in the earthly commonwealth." [16]

For all of these reasons, it is "expedient that good men should rule far and wide and long." [17] The problem, as noted above, is to find such men and to assist them in their rule. Augustine's pessimism in this regard should not be understood as fatalistic, nor should it blind one to the political potential of his teaching. In fact, his very pessimism is meant to open to his congregants and his readers a modicum of hope short of total social and political reformation. He suggests that it may make little difference under what ruler one lives in part to emphasize that *caritas* should exist in any kind of commonwealth. In fact, he does value social relations guided by *caritas* more highly than political relations. Yet he neither discounts the importance of good rule nor the kind of society that is required to support that good rule. On the contrary, his goal—as it was in his *Confessions*—is to create a more just social order. Like his Classical predecessors, he knew that only a good people could support good rule. Though he often counselled leaders and potential leaders, his fundamental task was clearly focused on the creation of civic virtue among ordinary persons without which his counsel to leaders would be quite meaningless.

Thus it seems that the most critical political task for Augustine is one that takes place outside of the formal political order. Indeed, the role of Roman political institutions as instruments of public instruction was and would remain decidedly limited. As Robert Markus notes:

In Augustine's mature thought there is no trace of a theory of the State
as concerned with man's self-fulfillment, perfection, the good life, felicity, or with "educating" man towards such purposes. Its function is more
restricted: it is to cancel out at least some of the evil effects of sin.
Political authority exists to resolve at least some of the tensions in human
society. [That is] . . . .Political authority serves to remedy the conflict,
tensions and disorder of society.[18]

Indeed the "relevant language of politics" was severely limited by Augustine who shunned the classical "politics of perfection." Religious
language and belief were necessary to help renew (though never to
perfect) some of the qualities of public virtue lost (or, for Augustine,
perhaps never present) in Rome. As he suggests in a letter to the Roman, Nectarius, "the greater is your desire to leave your country in a
safe and flourishing condition," the more seriously must be taken the
teachings of the church.

Away with all these vanities and follies, and let men be converted to the
true worship of God, and to chaste and pious manners: then will *you see
your country flourishing, not in the vain opinion of fools, but in the sound
judgment of the wise;* when your fatherland shall have become a portion
of that Fatherland into which we are born not by the flesh, but by faith.
. . . We are therefore resolved, neither on the one hand to lay aside
Christian gentleness, nor on the other to leave in your city that which
would be most pernicious for all others to follow [19] (emphasis added).

The job of moral instruction was, however, left to the church; that is,
to an institution less concerned with the organizational mandates of
control and power. The proximate order of the earthly city was, to a
significant degree, dependent upon the ability of the church to instruct
pilgrims and pagans [20] alike to unite in fellowship about objects truly
worthy of their affection.[21] The ability of the church to carry out that
instruction was on the other hand dependent on the ability of the state
to maintain a minimum of order and social cohesion. Here, of course,
the circle tightens, for order could not be maintained solely by coer-
cion. And one is led by Augustine to consider the relationship between
order and justice. That is, the more just the objects of common affection that bind a commonwealth together, the more orderly will that
commonwealth be.

The Bishop as Leader and Educator

"A bishop," said Augustine, "who loves preeminence not good works
should understand that he is no bishop." A bishop is guided by a

"compulsion of love," and led thereby to "undertake a righteous activity in affairs." [22] While his main tasks were not directly political, his role was fundamental to the substance of politics. In fact, located completely within the *saeculum,* the bishop's task was inevitably more relevant to ordinary politics than that of the prophets and priests—the great religious leaders and educators of the Old Testament. Christian bishops in their capacity as "watchmen . . . placed over the people" were charged with initiating through their good works a new order of things.[23]

Our priests, Augustine said, are not established to be worshiped as were those of ancient Egypt or the demons of Rome. Nor were Christian priests like those "after the order of Aaron." [24] Indeed, the priesthood of the New Testament is "the people itself, the people whose priest is the mediator between God and man, the man Christ Jesus." [25] The charge to the Christian ministry was to make Christ's example available and known to ordinary congregants, and thus to begin a renewal of spirit that would contribute to earthly peace, even as it praised the heavenly.

Christian education began in the family and in the church. Augustine's use of familial imagery in discussing political leaders introduces and suggests the importance of the education that takes place there. The family offers at least two critical moral/political lessons. In the first place, it can provide an example of just rule, whereby those who govern serve those they must command.[26] There, leadership can become the exercise of command "not through lust for rule but through dutiful concern for others, not with pride in exercising princely rule but with mercy in providing for others." The family can, however, provide more than an example of leadership. It can in addition contribute directly to the peace and harmony of the city, for the order of the household, said Augustine, is "the beginning . . . of the city." Indeed, "the ordered agreement among those who dwell together in a household ministers to the ordered agreement concerning command and obedience among citizens." [27]

Augustine understood with Aristotle that one who would rule had first to learn how to obey. Unlike Aristotle, however, Augustine felt that such basic instruction was best conducted apart from the interference of the state. For Augustine, Christian churches are "sacred seminaries of public instruction in which sound morality is inculcated and learned." The Christian minister through his instruction of parents and leaders and children and citizens had to instruct his congregants in those virtues, the prevalence of which in any city entitles it to be spoken of as flourishing in addition to teaching the worship of God. In

equally telling language, Augustine spoke of the use that the heavenly
city makes of the earthly peace, which

> guards and seeks the merging of human wills in regard to the things that
> are useful for man's mortal nature so far as sound piety and religion
> permit, and makes the earthly peace minister to the heavenly peace.[28]

Beginning with the family, Christian education extends to neighbor-
hoods, cities, and to entire peoples. Its goal at each stage is the creation
of peaceful and harmonious social relations. Indeed, the church seeks
to establish a reciprocal relationship between the two cities, recognizing
that the life of the two cities is and will remain intermingled on this
earth. In the end, the goal of the Christian educator is to influence the
very substance of the people to whom he speaks. A people, Augustine
defines, of course, as "a large gathering of rational beings united in
fellowship by their agreement about the objects of their love. . . ." [29]
The Christian religion, he suggests, offers an object to love that must
lead men to establish and maintain the best sort of fellowship.

Thus the Christian preacher comes to play a significant role in the
Augustinian theory of leadership. Just as Christ becomes the new
founder, and the Christian prince and magistrate the new stabilizer, so
the preacher/educator is an intermediary between the two. He offers
instruction that reminds both leaders and citizens of the founding example of Christ and so of the need to sustain and periodically renew
the *caritas* represented in His life. And so, the third leadership triad is
introduced as indicated in the following:

	Rome	Old Testament	Christian Era
Founder (Conditor)	Romulus/Numa	Abraham/Moses	Christ
Renewer (Magister)	Roman Hero	Old Testament Prophet	Augustinian Preacher
Stabilizer (Rex)	Ancient Kings	Davidic Kings	Christian Prince

The *magister*—a statesman in an age of crisis—is for Augustine separated from the duties of executing the public order. His task is twofold:
first, he must help to make that ordering more possible, and second, he
must strive to add such quality and substance to that order as are

possible given the restraints imposed by human nature. In the end, he has more ability to serve as an authoritative counsel, precisely because his role is more decisively separated from politics and its organizational necessities. Given that independence, he could develop a language and a doctrine more explicitly related to the lives and the most pressing problems of ordinary citizens.

It is not enough, says Augustine, merely to define the nature of the Christian prince and then offer him a "mirror of princes." In fact, he understood full well that the tasks of leadership are such that even a well-intentioned leader could forget first principles. Augustine's role as an intermediary or renewer thus looked both to the prince and the people in the fashion of the Old Testament prophet. There was at this time—given the influx of Romans into North Africa—a special need for public education.

Roman schools had been and remained inadequate. Augustine did not think that the state or its institutions could provide the needed education. Even the Christian prince was inadequate to the task at hand. What was needed was a prepolitical education that might allow men to come to terms with the most basic principles of their social existence. The church, thought Augustine, could provide an institutional framework in which such training could take place. To be sure, part of what is learned there is that men are alienated, imperfect beings and that political perfection is impossible. Augustine believed that he could offer a basis for clearer judgment that could help men confront such imperfection. The "fruit of his *Confessions*" did indeed stretch beyond his own personal changes. The psychological authority of that work could now be explicated in political terms.

The Need for Political Education

Genuine political reform requires a clear recognition of the capabilities of political man. Roman society had lost sight of these. Men had therefore to rethink the very nature of their human existence before they could understand what was wrong with Roman institutions, let alone reform them or create alternatives. Augustine left little doubt that men who engaged in such a reevaluation could make a difference. His insistence that only they could be effective reformers indicates the seriousness of his concern, not a lack of interest or hope in the possibility of change. The church's role thus became political or prepolitical as it helped to educate both Christian princes and Christian citizens.

The various strands of our argument thus begin to coalesce. Augustine's concerns with Roman North Africa are—broadly conceived—

political. As he confronted the fact of political decay in his critique of Rome, Augustine was forced to reexamine the foundations of social existence. Life in the city is a social life, which must be maintained in order for the city to survive. Social life can, however, take a number of forms, and some of them are stronger than others. In order to survive, the city must maintain its social life.

The clues, he insists, to the maintenance of that social life are to be found in that event that originally brought the men of the city together. As men lose sight of their origins, they lose sight of that which was socially formative. The city as a unit may remain, but its unity comes to depend on ever-shifting objects of common affection. Social harmony is now less formidable, for shifting objects of affection create shifting coalitions of support for those objects. Divisiveness grows, and men increasingly turn inward and either protect that which is theirs or submit to someone who will protect it for them. In either case, men lose their freedom. They become the victims of their possessions in the first case and the subjects of their masters in the second. Freedom can in turn be gained or regained only in concert with one's fellows—only through the social life of the city and a recognition of the limits which that life imposes on private desires.

Insofar as he recognizes his natural dependence, man is in a position to work out his own survival. In an interesting way then, Augustine argues that man's most fundamental nature—when recognized—leads him to politics. Even men who had been intimidated by the exalted demands of Roman heroism might, under the right circumstances, act together on the basis of shared feelings, in pursuit of their common good.

The problem was that Roman culture clouded the true nature of both alienation and dependence. Augustine must, therefore, first reawaken his listeners to their natural condition and then motivate them to live their lives more justly. The task is prima facie a very demanding one. He asked people accustomed to heroic standards consciously to accept their own limits and those of all human beings as well. To avoid such a confrontation with one's self was to avoid, even to deny, one's very nature. It was as well a denial of those essential truths that were the bases of justice and the just political life.

This is surely a reversal of the normal approach to Augustine that correctly emphasizes his description of sinful man in need of the restrictions of government. Augustine makes such arguments, but he goes beyond this restricted conception of politics as well. Man—alienated, sinful, and dependent—has on occasion come to terms with the fact of his condition, and something very different from the decay of Rome has resulted. Augustine investigated those alternatives—primarily in the

Old Testament—and probed the source of their spirit. He placed himself in militant confrontation with those who would, in denying the significance of such probing, eliminate the possibility of rediscovering the social life that is the basis of the city. Only through this rediscovery could the earthly peace minister to the needs of the heavenly city.

The *City of God* is an attempt to provide a perspective through which men could view the particulars of their everyday lives. Sheldon Wolin is partially correct in noting Augustine's seeming preference for the social over the political. "The one," Wolin says, "connoted harmonious fellowship, the other conflict and domination." [30] Augustine was indeed wary of political institutions because of their contamination by conflict and domination, still, he thought that conflict was inevitable within this life, and that when it was absent, something was wrong. He sought then not to eliminate all conflict, but to direct conflict more carefully than had the Romans. Men could do battle together against common external enemies who challenged their integrity. They could guard against common temptation from within their society or from within themselves, or they could battle among themselves to see who would dominate. True peace would never come, but the right kind of battle could be fought. Without the perspective of the *City of God,* Augustine thought that men would all too easily lapse into a conflict that seemed easier but that was in the end self-defeating. The evidence around him was clear. It was his task to confront the antipolitics of Rome, not with the politics of the church but with the new perspective through which men could judge Rome. He offered an analysis that at once exposed Rome and prepared men to confront common problems with a clearer sense of that which they shared.

Political Theory as Public Confession

Augustine praised Plato for having united the two branches of the pursuit of wisdom—practical and theoretical.

> The first is concerned with the conduct of life, that is to say with the shaping of morals; the second with the discovery of natural principles and truth in its purest form. Socrates is said to have excelled in the former, while Pythagoras on the other hand bent all his intellectual strength rather to the theoretical side. Hence Plato is extolled because he united the two branches and so perfected philosophy. . . . [31]

Augustine sought the same "ordered agreement of knowledge and action which," he says, "we called the peace of the rational soul." [32] That peace is, of course, an active peace.

Men will, however, need special instruction to reach this point. The education of God's people and that of each individual in these matters are parallel.

> The true education of the human race, at least as far as God's people were concerned was like that of an individual. It advanced by steps in time, as the individual does when a new stage of life is reached. Thus it mounted from the level of temporal things to a level where it could grasp the eternal, and from visible things to a grasp of invisibles.[33]

What was important was that at each step along the way the individual had a perspective from which to view his actions and chart his directions. Self-delusion was a regular danger. The only antidote was, and for Augustine remained, an unending search for self-knowledge—the search in which he was engaged and in which he tried to engage all who would follow.

At each stage the individual will face new threats to his freedom.

> The first period of his life, that is, infancy, is subject to the flesh without struggle, and the second, which is called childhood, when reason has not yet taken up the battle, is at the mercy of almost all sinful pleasures. For, though that age has a power of speech . . . its weakness of discernment is not yet able to keep the commandment of God. . . . But when the age is reached that is able to keep the commandment and to be subject to the rule of law, a man must take up war against the vices and wage it vigorously. . . .[34]

The stages of the *City of God* are thus united with those of the *Confessions*. The *Confessions* introduces the *City of God* in that it aims at preparing men for "that age that is able to keep the commandment." The *City of God* extends and even fulfills the *Confessions* with the insistence that an individual could not be satisfied solely with a retreat into the recesses of his mind—for in the end, Augustine argued in his *Confessions* that "I will pass beyond this power of mine which is called memory." [35] In addition, men must be taught to confront their world with an understanding of its history and its politics. Men will recognize, Augustine hoped, the urgency of the battle they face as they come to a better understanding of themselves. Combatting temptation will in turn strengthen that very self-knowledge. Augustine sought to play a significant role in the initiation of this process of self-awareness.

Self-awareness would come to guide our understanding of others and help push toward the end of the creation of human peace. Again the task of education is to provide a constant perspective from which to view one's actions. If a man recognizes his limitations as well as his potential, he will be at peace with himself and, with all men in that human peace or ordered agreement, of which the pattern is this: first, to do harm to no man, and secondly, to help every man that he can. In the first place, then, he has the care of his own household, inasmuch as the order of nature or of human society provides him with a readier and easier access to them for seeking their interest. Wherefore the Apostle says: "Whosoever does not provide for his own, and especially for those of his household he denies the faith and is worse than the infidel." [36]

Thus, says Augustine, the concern of the church for the peace of mind of an individual is likewise shown to be a concern for his relations with other people. The instruction offered is thus social and religious. Insofar as it creates a people and peace in the *saeculum,* it is political as well.

Augustine had little hope for total peace, but he thought that its approximation should be sought with great energy. The first step was to develop the self-discipline and endurance of individuals. In recognizing their limits, men could begin ordering their lives by governing that which is closest to them. In a piece of advice that is lost on much of the remainder of the Middle Ages, he suggests that men aim first at those tasks that they can hope to achieve. An individual had first to learn to rule himself and learn to obey that rule before he could learn effectively to be ruled and to rule. Political authority could not be understood until personal authority had been established.

Augustine thus faced the problems of political change and political leadership on several levels at once. He was concerned with educating both Christian citizens and Christian leaders. He saw the development of the individual and a people as complementary with both in need of appropriate leadership. Finally, and most significantly for Augustine himself, he saw the need for the teacher—*magister,* mediator, renewer— who is charged with keeping people and their leaders constantly alert so that they might pursue those goals that they have come to share.

The church in this context became an important institutional focus, for it afforded each man a place to reflect; a setting—the congregation— in which he gathered with others; and an institution through which he and his fellows renewed that which they shared. Such roles need not be explicitly political. The church was, however, probably the only available source of public regard. Augustine hoped that it could provide a framework within which men could once again recognize public virtue—that it might in turn initiate true public action.

The church became, for Augustine, very much a part of the *saeculum*—of "the world of men and of time." Leaders of the church were, as well, a part of that world. They had, therefore, the responsibility to act within it to further the end of public virtue, of a "rightly ordered love." Augustine had learned of the difficulties of such action. His own experiences had taught him that confession of sin and praise might lead to a new respect for public purpose. He sought, as one of the leaders of his church and so of the *saeculum,* to elicit that respect from others. His political action and his political thought were thus united in his own public posture—a posture of public confession.

Notes

1. *DCD,* XVII, 4.
2. Wolin, p. 100.
3. *DCD,* XVII, 4. Augustine's plea to execute "judgment in the midst of the earth" becomes possible precisely because of God's direct intervention in Roman history.
4. Ibid., XXII, 6.
5. Cited in *Saeculum,* p. 149.
6. Ibid.
7. Ibid., XVII, 11.
8. Ibid., II, 21.
9. "Epistle 138," *Nicene and Post-Nicene Fathers of the Christian Church,* vol. I, Wm. B. Eerdmans Publishing Co., Grand Rapids, Michigan, 1956, p. 484.
10. See *Saeculum.* Robert Markus' brilliant study convincingly opens for our attention those more positive aspects of Augustine's understanding of the "history of human societies."
11. "De Utilitate Credendi," Migne, vol. 42, p. 85.
12. Cited in Peter Brown, *Politics and Society,* p. 34.
13. *DCD,* V, 24.
14. *Epistle 133,* p. 470.
15. *Epistle 138,* p. 485.
16. Ibid., pp. 486–87. Herbert Deane has suggested that here and in the *City of God* (II, 19) Augustine speaks of conditions contrary to fact. Augustine is led, Deane notes, to counsel Christians "to suffer the burden of this Republic, wicked and most vicious though it be. . . ." He continues the preceding observation, however, with the comment—*"if so it must be."* He was not, of course, naively optimistic about an alternative society, but neither did he fatalistically resign himself to Roman society. The letter cited here is one of many clear examples of that fact. *DCD* II, 19.
17. *DCD,* IV, 3.
18. Markus, pp. 94–95.
19. *Epistle 91,* Ch. 6.
20. Ibid., Ch. 10.
21. *DCD,* XIX, 24.
22. Ibid., XIX, 19.
23. Ibid., I, 9.
24. Ibid., VIII, 27.
25. Ibid.

26. Ibid., XIX, 14.
27. Ibid., XIX, 16.
28. Ibid., XIX, 17.
29. Ibid., XIX, 24.
30. Wolin, p. 130.
31. *DCD*, VIII, 4.
32. Ibid., XIX, 14.
33. Ibid., X, 14.
34. Ibid., XXI, 16.
35. *Confs.*, X, 17.
36. *DCD*, XIX, 14.

Index

Abraham, 144-48, 151; as mediator, 146
Affection, 45-48
Allard, G.H., 122, 129n.
Alypius, 49-50, 52, 110-11
Ambrose, St., 25, 41-42, 46, 52-53, 70, 75
Amor dei, 85, 89
Amor sui, 85
Anxiety, 37, 39-43, 59-60; negative to positive, 51-54
Aristotle, 161
Auctoritas, 119-20
Authority: and anxiety, 39-43; parental, 45; search for, 120-22

Bishop, as leader and educator, 160-63
Bonum, omnium, 90-91
Bright, John, 5, 13n.
Brown, Peter, xii, 1, 12n., 13n., 55n., 113n., 115n., 128n.
Burnaby, John, 86, 90, 93n.
Burrell, David, 98, 114n.

Caritas, 3, 20, 23, 27, 39, 40, 42, 65-68, 73, 76, 81-95, 135, 159
Carnal affection, 45-47, 52

Carnal anxiety, 69-72, 74, 144
Christ, Jesus, 26, 155; as mediator, 26-28; conversion to, 54; death of, 73
Christian education: principles of, 2-3, 81, 99, 161-63; and inner-world ascetism, 111-14
Christianity, 69
Christian leaders, 157-60
Churches, 161-62
Cicero, 13n., 14n., 52, 131
City of God, xii, 10-12, 19, 31, 41, 83, 87, 100, 105, 113, 119-20, 124, 143, 149, 151, 158, 166
Cochrane, Charles Norris, 14n.
Community, 87-89, 155
Confessions, xii, 10-12, 15-31, 35-46, 49, 52, 59-76, 101, 103, 111, 120, 149, 152; Book VIII, 67-69; Book IX, 69-72; Book X, 62-65; Book XI, 65-66; Book XII, 66-67
Confessional teaching, 7-10, 64
Confessio laudis, 21, 22
Confessio peccati, 21
Constantius II, 1
"Corrosive anxieties," 41-42
Covenantal foundation of society, 131

171